the sweet life

101 indulgent recipes made with SPLENDA® sweetener

the sweet life

101 indulgent recipes made with SPLENDA® sweetener

antony worrall thompson

FALL RIVER PRESS

photography by steve baxter

Acknowledgements

To my wife Jacinta and our children Toby and Billie who helped me with the enjoyable task of trying all the recipes in this book.

To the team at Splenda with whom I have worked closely for many years now, developing delicious recipes, without the sugar. To the team at Hill & Knowlton for their help in making this book a success.

To Sue Ashworth and Joanna Farrow who tested the recipes and worked their way through many boxes of Splenda in the process! To Steve Baxter, his assistant Delphine Bodart, and props stylist Rachel Jukes for the beautiful images. To my publisher, Kyle Cathie, for taking on this exciting project. To my editor, Suzanna de Jong, and the team at Kyle Cathie Ltd. for making this fantastic book in no time at all.

Photography © Splenda (McNeil Nutritionals Ltd. 2008), except for p. 7 © Alan Strutt and Melinda Messenger, and p. 9 © Harry Borden
Book design © 2008 Kyle Cathie Limited

Text © 2008 Antony Worrall Thompson, except for pp. 14, 18, 20, 24, 39, 46, 50, 54, 60, 61, 67, 86, 90, 103, 104, 109, 117-132, 135, 136, 142, 146, 150, 156, 159, 160, 164, 167, 168 and 171 © Splenda (McNeil Nutritionals Ltd. 2008)

Editor: Suzanna de Jong
Designer: Geoff Hayes
Photographer: Steve Baxter
Editorial Assistant: Julia Gelpke
Home Economist: Sue Ashworth
Prop Stylist: Rachel Jukes
Recipe Analysis: Wendy Doyle
Production: Sha Huxtable

SPLENDA® is the licensed trademark of McNeil Nutritionals, LLC

Fall River Press
122 Fifth Avenue
New York, NY 10011

ISBN 978-1-4351-1549-1

Printed and bound in China by C&C Offset

1 3 5 7 9 10 8 6 4 2

contents

foreword

Calling all dessert lovers!

A balanced diet and regular exercise are important aspects of my life, making me feel healthier and helping me to stay in shape. But as a busy Mum with three kids, my days are hectic and the gym is often a distant memory, so meal times become my main focus.

Meal times give me a chance to catch up with the kids on all the excitement of the day while making sure we've all had a healthy, nutritious meal. And guess what? That doesn't mean all desserts go out of the window! So what's my secret to delicious, homemade desserts that I'm happy for all the family to enjoy? Well, it's all thanks to Antony Worrall Thompson.

I've known Antony for several years and have always adored his cooking, so I've often asked him for tips and advice. The best tip he's ever given me is to substitute SPLENDA® sweetner for sugar where I can. It's the perfect way to make hundreds of delicious desserts without all the calories of sugar. By taking his advice, I can make lighter desserts that are better for my waistline and healthier for my family, but still taste great.

When it comes to weekends, my kitchen is always buzzing. The whole family piles in and the kids always insist that we bake together. Despite the mess, this is my favorite way to spend the day and we've tried lots of sweet recipes using Splenda sweetener instead of sugar. The kids can't even tell the difference.

Providing I've got the time, I can also be pretty adventurous in the kitchen if I'm entertaining. When dessert is on the menu and my friends find out that

they've been made with sweetener instead of sugar, guess who's the popular one!

I was delighted when Antony asked me to contribute eight of my favorite recipes to this book. The recipes that I've chosen are favorites with me, my friends, and, most importantly, my kids. Ranging from an everyday Apple Pie and tasty Chocolate Brownies, to a delicious Tiramisù and Christmas Punch, they are all low in sugar and so simple to make.

So go on, what are you waiting for, get cooking and enjoy these delicious treats!

Love,
Melinda Messenger

introduction

Baking and making your own desserts seems to be a dying practice in many homes these days—what a shame. I have fond childhood memories of sitting around the table as a family, eating a homemade cake or dessert. It was such a treat, and I feel that, actually, all of us should get to enjoy a bit of sweetness now and again, after dinner or as a snack.

Unfortunately, children spend a lot of their time sitting down nowadays, in front of the TV, at the computer, or with a Game Boy. Adults aren't much better really, using the car for errands and shopping, and claiming we're too busy to go to the gym. The fact is we don't get nearly enough exercise and this makes it hard to sustain a healthy, old-fashioned diet.

Obesity is a growing problem in adults and children alike, and something our generation needs to deal with. It's vital to our health that we find ways to reduce our daily calorific intake, but at the same time, it is equally important that we continue to enjoy the food we eat! Food is not just about health, and it's not about excluding any particular food groups or ingredients. It's all about balance.

Sugar as a food group is one that you can easily cut back on in my opinion. Sugar gives you energy, but our bodies can get all the energy they need from other carbohydrates as well, so you don't need to consume that much sugar at all. But, and this is a big but, many of us thoroughly enjoy sweet things, and we mustn't deny ourselves satisfying those sweet cravings. Enter SPLENDA® sweetener. By replacing with Splenda some, if not most, of the sugar you add to your food, you can reduce the calorie intake of your family.

I started using Splenda sweetener myself when I found out I was heading towards diabetes. My resistance to insulin, a hormone that helps the body to process sugar and use it as fuel, was so high that I was at risk of developing diabetes. I had to take drastic steps to reduce my weight. But, as a chef, I want to cook my family the food that they love to eat. By using Splenda sweetener, I have managed to do both—reduce the amount of sugar I eat while still cooking delicious things.

The fantastic thing about Splenda, giving it the thumbs up over some other sweeteners on the market, is that it can be used in cooking and baking. I've tried many different sweeteners over the years, only to become frustrated. While perfectly suitable to stir into your tea and coffee, or to sprinkle over your cereal, I couldn't use them for the thing I like best: cooking.

The recipes in this book full of sweet things use Splenda sweetener rather than sugar where possible. This doesn't mean there's no sugar in them at all—I've still used ingredients that contain natural sugars such as fruit, and some of the baking recipes need a little bit of sugar, honey, or syrup to make them work. However, the sugar content has been cut down as much as possible for each and every recipe and, remember, when it comes to controlling your weight, every little bit helps. If you have diabetes, you'll know through your doctor or nutritionist what you can and cannot eat. I've added nutritional information at the end of each recipe to help you make the right choice for you.

So here's to enjoying sweetness again—as part of a healthy, balanced lifestyle.

all about SPLENDA® sweetener

What is Splenda sweetener?

If you're looking to reduce the amount of sugar in your diet without compromising on taste, then there is an easy way: with SPLENDA® No Calorie Sweetener, which is made from sugar, tastes like sugar, but it's not sugar.

SPLENDA® Brand Sweeteners are available in a variety of forms and can be used as tasty alternatives to sugar. Unlike some other sweeteners, Splenda is heat stable and keeps its delicious sweet taste at high temperatures, making it the perfect alternative to sugar when cooking and baking.

You can use Splenda no calorie sweetener spoon for spoon like sugar and reduce the number of calories you consume. Splenda no calorie sweetener has the sweet taste you want without all of sugar's calories.

Splenda sweetener and diabetes

Splenda is suitable for people with diabetes to use as part of a healthy, balanced diet. Sucralose, the sweetening ingredient in Splenda, is not metabolized by the body. As a result, Splenda has an insignificant effect on insulin or blood glucose levels. This means that by replacing sugar with Splenda sweetener, even people with diabetes can enjoy sweet dishes and baked treats.

Tips for cooking and baking with Splenda sweetener

When cooking and baking, it is useful to keep in mind that Splenda works best in recipes where sugar is used to provide a sweet taste, like in pie fillings, sweet sauces, and glazes. Try replacing every $1/3$ cup sugar with about 8 tablespoons of Splenda. It's a good idea to start with a little less Splenda and taste the dish as you go, to see how sweet you like it. For cooking and baking with Splenda, just follow the guidelines below to get great results, without all the calories.

Mixing

There are three ways to successfully incorporate Splenda sweetener into a recipe:

✳ Combine thoroughly with other dry ingredients
✳ Dissolve in liquid
✳ Cream with butter or other fat

Sifting

Splenda does not sift like sugar, so if a recipe calls for sifting the dry ingredients, measure the amount of sweetener you need and add it to the other ingredients after sifting.

Creaming

Often when you're baking, the recipe calls for creaming ingredients, such as butter, sugar, and eggs, together. With Splenda, you may need to beat the ingredients a little longer to get enough air into the mixture—that way you'll end up with a more fluffy and even texture.

Cooking

Check your baked goodies 7 to 10 minutes before the end of the suggested cooking time (1 to 2 minutes before for cookies) as some products cook more quickly with Splenda. To make sure a cake is cooked on the inside, just insert a skewer into the middle of the cake—it should come out clean. If it's still sticky, cook it for a little longer.

Storing

Products made with Splenda may not last as long as products made with sugar, since sugar acts as a preservative as well as a sweetener. You can make your Splenda products last longer by storing them in airtight containers in the fridge. Most can also be frozen for even longer storage.

For additional tips and advice on Splenda visit www.splenda.com

baked treats

summer berry phyllo slice

SERVES 6

vegetable oil, for greasing

five 14 x 18-inch sheets phyllo
   pastry dough

3½ tablespoons butter, melted

1¼ cups heavy cream

scant cup raspberries

scant cup blackberries

2 tablespoons Splenda granulated
   sweetener

1 cup strawberries, hulled and sliced

This lovely summer dessert uses phyllo pastry dough—rather than puff pastry dough—to make a lighter version of a mille feuille.

Preheat the oven to 400°F. Lightly grease 3 baking trays with a little vegetable oil. (If you only have one or two baking trays, you can bake the pastry in batches).

Place one sheet of phyllo dough on a clean counter and brush with melted butter. Pile the rest of the phyllo dough sheets on top, brushing each separate sheet with melted butter as you go. Use a sharp knife or scissors to cut the pile into three stacks, each measuring about 14 x 6 inches. Place each stack onto a baking tray.

Bake the phyllo stacks in the oven for 5–6 minutes, or until golden brown. Remove from the oven and let cool completely.

Whip the cream in a chilled bowl until it forms soft peaks. Crush half the raspberries and blackberries lightly with a fork and add the sweetener. Fold lightly through the cream–there is no need to mix them in thoroughly.

Put one stack of phyllo sheets onto a serving platter. Spread half the cream mixture over the surface and scatter half the fruit on top. Place another stack of phyllo sheets on top, then carefully spoon the rest of the cream mixture over them. Add the remaining fruit, and top with the last stack of phyllo sheets. Chill until ready to serve.

Per serving: 380 calories; 3g protein; 35g fat; 19.6g saturated fat; 14g carbohydrates; 4.6g sugar; 1.1g fiber; 0.21g sodium

baked cheesecake with marsala-steeped raisins

SERVES 10

scant cup raisins

⅓ cup marsala

3 tablespoons unsalted butter, plus extra for greasing

18 squares (9 sheets) graham crackers, crushed

1¾ (14 ounces) regular cream cheese

1¼ cups plain yogurt

⅔ cup light cream

½ cup Splenda granulated sweetener

2 teaspoons vanilla extract

3 eggs, beaten

Unlike many baked cheesecakes, this version is smooth and creamy but not too heavy. The secret of achieving a creamy soft, set center is to bake it until lightly set around the edges but still very wobbly when you gently shake the pan.

Preheat the oven to 350°F. Put the raisins and marsala in a small saucepan and heat until bubbling around the edges. Remove from the heat and let stand while preparing the cheesecake mixture.

Grease the sides of an 8-inch cake pan with a removable bottom. Melt the butter and mix with the crushed graham crackers until they start to bind together. Scoop into the pan and pack them down with the back of a spoon.

Using a hand-held electric beater, beat the cream cheese in a bowl until softened. Add the yogurt, cream, sweetener, vanilla extract, eggs, and any unabsorbed marsala from the pan. Beat until smooth. Turn the mixture into the pan and scatter the top with the raisins.

Bake in the oven for about 35–40 minutes, or until the surface is pale golden and set around the edges but the cake still wobbles when the pan is shaken gently. Loosen the edges with a knife and let cool in the pan before unhinging the sides and transferring to a serving plate.

Per serving: 369 calories; 6g protein; 30g fat; 17.8g saturated fat; 17g carbohydrates; 9.8g sugar; 0.4g fiber; 0.28g sodium

apple and almond puff slices

MAKES 8

butter, for greasing
13 ounces ready-rolled puff pastry,
thawed if frozen
1 cup ground almonds
3 tablespoons Splenda granulated
  sweetener
1 egg, beaten
2 eating apples, cored and thinly sliced
¹⁄₃ cup slivered almonds

These heavenly pastries are simplicity itself to make. Serve them warm with a generous spoonful of Greek-style yogurt.

Preheat the oven to 400°F. Lightly grease two baking trays.

Unroll the pastry sheets and cut out eight circles using a 3½-inch biscuit cutter. Place four circles onto each baking tray.

Mix the almonds with the sweetener, adding just enough beaten egg to make a fairly stiff paste. Put a tablespoonful of the mixture in the middle of each circle and spread it out a little.

Arrange the apple slices neatly on top of the almond mixture. Brush the pastry with the remaining beaten egg. Sprinkle with the slivered almonds.

Bake in the oven for 12–15 minutes, until the pastries are puffed up and golden brown. Cool for about 10 minutes, then serve warm. The slices are lovely with some Greek-style yogurt.

Per serving: 302 calories; 7g protein; 21g fat; 5.3g saturated fat; 22g carbohydrates; 5.1g sugar; 1.7g fiber; 0.16g sodium

anzac cookies

½ cup (1 stick) unsalted butter, cut into
   cubes, plus extra for greasing
¾ cup rolled oats (old-fashioned oats)
1 cup dried coconut
¾ cup all-purpose flour
⅓ cup Splenda granulated sweetener
1 teaspoon baking soda
2 teaspoons ground ginger
2 tablespoons golden syrup (or corn
   syrup)

These chunky, crumbly cookies are ready to eat in half an hour.

Preheat the oven to 350°F. Grease a large cookie sheet. Mix the oats, coconut, flour, sweetener, baking soda, and ginger in a bowl.

Melt the butter with the golden syrup in a small saucepan. Pour the mixture over the dry ingredients and stir together until combined.

Divide the mixture into 12 equal-sized balls. Place on the cookie sheet and flatten, spacing the cookies slightly apart. Bake for 10–12 minutes until slightly risen and golden. Transfer to a wire rack to cool.

Per serving: 173 calories; 2g protein; 12g fat; 8.4g saturated fat; 14g carbohydrates; 3.4g sugar; 1.8g fiber; 0.12g sodium

shortbread

SERVES 8

½ cup (1 stick) cold butter, cubed, plus
   extra for greasing
1⅓ cups all-purpose flour
3 heaping tablespoons Splenda
   granulated sweetener
1 teaspoon almond extract (optional)

Sue Lancaster won the Splenda Recipe Club competition with this delicious recipe for sugar-free shortbread.

Preheat the oven to 350°F. Grease an 8-inch baking pan with a little butter. Rub together the flour, butter, sweetener, and almond extract, if using, into a dough. Wrap in plastic wrap and chill in the fridge for at least 15 minutes. Put the dough into the baking pan and push it to flatten and fill the pan. Prick the dough all over with a fork and bake for 15–20 minutes until lightly golden. Let cool, then serve.

Per serving: 184 calories; 2g protein; 12g fat; 7.5g saturated fat; 18g carbohydrates; 1.1g sugar; 0.7g fiber; 0.09g sodium

plum and marzipan phyllo tarts

SERVES 6

6 phyllo pastry dough sheets, thawed
   if frozen
6½ tablespoons (scant ½ cup)
   delicately flavored olive oil
⅓ cup marzipan, grated
6 large plums, pitted and sliced
¼ cup Splenda granulated sweetener
Greek-style plain yogurt or whipped
   cream, for serving

These wonderful fruit-filled tarts are equally tasty with sliced apples instead of plums.

Preheat the oven to 375°F.

Unfold the 6 phyllo pastry sheets and lay them flat on top of each other. Cut through all six layers to form six squares, each measuring about 4 x 4 inches. Layer these phyllo squares into six individual tartlet molds, brushing each pastry sheet with a little olive oil.

Sprinkle an equal amount of grated marzipan on each tartlet mold. Toss the sliced plums with the sweetener, then divide them between the tartlet molds.

Bake for 10–12 minutes until the plums are tender and the pastry is golden brown. Cool slightly, then serve with yogurt or whipped cream.

Per serving: 303 calories; 3g protein; 18g fat; 2.4g saturated fat; 34g carbohydrates; 20.2g sugar; 1.6g fiber; 0.23g sodium

cheat's baklava

SERVES 8

for the filling:
1½ cups pine nuts
7 ounces (scant cup) soft cheese
   (e.g., cream cheese)
½ teaspoon ground cloves
1 tablespoon honey
1 teaspoon Splenda granulated
   sweetener

1 pound phyllo pastry dough
melted butter, for brushing
honey, for drizzling
⅓ cup pine nuts, toasted and chopped

This recipe is from my BBC *Saturday Brunch* show. Making it the traditional Greek way is long and fiddly but this version works well and is easy to do in less than 30 minutes. I love the sugary, spicy flavors of good baklava.

Preheat the oven to 350°F. For the filling, mix all the ingredients together in a bowl and set aside.

Unfold the phyllo pastry dough and, using a sharp knife, carefully cut into thirds. Take two pieces at a time and fold in half. Brush with melted butter. Keeping the narrow end towards you, take some of the filling and spread it over the folded dough, keeping a border free along all sides. Fold the sides in to cover the filling and roll up. Repeat with the remaining pastry dough and filling.

Place the rolls on a greased baking sheet and brush the rolled pastries generously with butter. Bake for 10–15 minutes or until golden brown. Serve the baklava with a drizzle of honey and the toasted pine nuts scattered on top.

Per serving: 632 calories; 11g protein; 50g fat; 19.3g saturated fat; 39g carbohydrates; 7.3g sugar; 0.6g fiber; 0.73g sodium

macaroons

1 teaspoon vegetable oil
¾ cup whole blanched almonds
²/₃ cup dried coconut
2 egg whites
½ teaspoon cream of tartar
2 tablespoons sugar
3 tablespoons Splenda granulated
  sweetener

When ground almonds are a focal ingredient in a recipe, it's best to use whole blanched almonds and grind them in a food processor to bring out their flavor, though you can use store-bought ground almonds as a time saver.

Preheat the oven to 350°F. Line a large baking sheet with parchment paper and brush with the oil.

Reserve 12 of the almonds and grind the rest in a food processor. Add the coconut and blend again until the coconut is partially ground.

Using a hand-held electric beater, beat the egg whites in a thoroughly clean bowl until foamy. Add the cream of tartar and beat again until stiff. Mix together the caster sugar and sweetener and gradually whisk into the egg whites, a teaspoonful at a time.

Tip the ground nuts into the beaten whites and fold in using a large metal spoon. Place spoonfuls of the mixture on the baking sheet, spacing them slightly apart. Place a whole almond on each macaroon and bake for 12–15 minutes until golden. Transfer to a wire rack to cool.

Per serving: 90 calories; 2g protein; 7g fat; 2.6g saturated fat; 3g carbohydrates; 3.2g sugar; 1.2g fiber; 0.07g sodium

fruit, nut, and seed bars

MAKES 12

¾ cup (1½ sticks) butter, plus extra for
   greasing
²/₃ cup honey
¹/₃ cup Splenda granulated sweetener
2 cups rolled oats (old fashioned oats)
pinch of salt
7 ounces fruit and nut mixture (dried
apricots, raisins or golden raisins,
   cashews and coconut shavings
   are nice)
¹/₃ cup dried cranberries
½ cup mixed seeds (like sunflower,
   pumpkin, and flax seeds)
²/₃ cup dried coconut

**These energy bars are just the thing for a mid-morning boost, and
they're a perfect fit for a packed lunch or picnic.**

Preheat the oven to 350°F. Grease an 8-inch square baking pan and line with
parchment paper, leaving an overhang to make it easier to remove the bars later.

Melt the butter and honey in a large saucepan over a gentle heat. Bring to a boil
and cook for 2 minutes, stirring constantly. Remove from the heat.

Mix together the sweetener, oats, salt, fruit and nut mixture, cranberries, mixed
seeds, and coconut. Add to the saucepan and stir together until thoroughly
mixed. Tip into the prepared pan and level the surface with the back of a spoon.

Bake in the oven for 25–30 minutes until golden brown. Cool for 30 minutes,
then remove from the pan and cut into 12 bars. Cool completely on a wire rack.
Keep in an airtight container.

Per serving: 337 calories; 6g protein; 19g fat; 10.6g saturated fat; 37g carbohydrates;
17.3g sugar; 4.8g fiber; 0.16g sodium

date, walnut, and lemon cookies

MAKES 14

5 tablespoons (¾ stick) lightly salted butter, cut into cubes, plus extra for greasing

1 cup dates

1 cup walnuts

1 tablespoon honey

finely grated zest of 1 lemon

¾ cup steel-cut oats

3 tablespoons all-purpose flour

3 tablespoons Splenda granulated sweetener

1 teaspoon vanilla extract

1 egg, beaten

extra steel-cut oats, for dusting

These little cookies are golden on the outside, yet slightly soft in the center—perfect for a reasonably healthy snack to serve with tea or coffee. They'd also work well with other firm—textured dried fruit such as figs, or with any other nuts.

Preheat the oven to 425°F. Grease a large baking sheet. Whizz the dates in a food processor until chopped into small pieces. Add the walnuts and blend again until chopped.

Melt the butter in a medium saucepan with the honey and lemon zest. Tip in the dates and walnuts, steel-cut oats, flour, sweetener, and vanilla, and stir until mixed. Add the egg and beat to a thick paste.

Take spoonfuls of the mixture and shape into balls. Flatten onto the baking sheet, spacing them slightly apart. Sprinkle with extra steel-cut oats and bake for 10 minutes or until golden brown around the edges. Transfer to a wire rack to cool.

Per serving: 153 calories; 3g protein; 9g fat; 3.4g saturated fat; 16g carbohydrates; 8.8g sugar; 1.2g fiber; 0.03g sodium

apricot and ginger teabread

SERVES 12

1$\frac{1}{3}$ cups ready-to-eat dried apricots,
chopped

2 pieces preserved ginger in syrup,
finely chopped

$\frac{1}{3}$ cup raisins

1$\frac{1}{4}$ cups orange juice

$\frac{1}{2}$ teaspoon vegetable or sunflower oil

1$\frac{2}{3}$ cups self-rising flour

$\frac{1}{2}$ cup Splenda granulated sweetener

2 eggs, beaten

Melinda says: I love apricots and I love ginger and the combination in this recipe is out of this world. The perfect accompaniment to a cup of coffee after a long day's work.

Mix together the apricots, preserved ginger, raisins, and orange juice, and let soak for 30 minutes. Use the oil to grease a 9x5x3-inch loaf pan. Line the pan with baking parchment (or dust the pan with flour).

Preheat the oven to 350°F. Sift the flour into a large bowl and stir in the sweetener.

Beat the eggs into the apricot mixture. Make a well in the middle of the flour and add the apricot mixture gradually, beating to make a batter. Pour into the prepared pan and bake for 45 minutes until golden.

To make sure the teabread is cooked, insert a skewer into the center. If it comes out clean, the bread is done. If not, bake for a little longer. Let cool in the pan for 10 minutes, then place on a wire rack to cool completely. Serve in slices.

The teabread is suitable for freezing. It can be stored in an airtight container in the fridge for three to four days.

Per serving: 135 calories; 4g protein; 1g fat; 0.4g saturated fat; 29g carbohydrates; 14.6g sugar; 2g fiber; 0.09g sodium

coconut, apricot, and passionfruit slices

SERVES 12

¾ cup (1½ sticks) unsalted butter,
  softened, plus extra for greasing
¹/₃ cup creamed coconut
½ cup Splenda granulated
  sweetener
3 eggs, beaten
½ cup all-purpose flour
1 teaspoon baking powder
pinch of salt
2 teaspoons vanilla extract
1¼ cups dried coconut
3½ ounces (½-²/₃ cup) ready-to-eat
dried apricots, chopped

for the glaze:
¹/₃ cup ready-to-eat dried apricots,
  chopped
¹/₃ cup freshly squeezed orange juice
2 passionfruit cut in half
1 teaspoon Splenda granulated
  sweetener
coconut shavings, lightly toasted, for
  decoration

This simple fruit slice recipe is a tempting combination of coconut and naturally sweet, fruity flavors. It's best served on the day you make it as both the cake and topping will dry out overnight. To make the coconut shavings for the topping, pare strips of flesh from a fresh coconut and toast them lightly under a hot broiler.

Preheat the oven to 350°F. Grease and line an 8 x 10-inch shallow, rectangular baking pan with parchment paper or foil.

Put the butter, creamed coconut and sweetener in a bowl and beat with a hand-held electric beater until pale and creamy. (If the creamed coconut is very firm, you can soften it first in the microwave.) Gradually beat in the eggs, one at a time, beating well after each addition. Sift the flour, baking powder, and salt into the bowl and stir in along with the vanilla, coconut, and chopped apricots.

Turn the batter into the pan and level the surface. Bake for 25 minutes until just firm to the touch.

Meanwhile, make the glaze. Heat the apricots and orange juice in a small saucepan for 5 minutes. Tip into a food processor and scoop out and add the pulp from the passionfruit and the sweetener. Blend until smooth.

Transfer the cake to a cooling rack and let cool. Using a spoon, drizzle the apricot and passionfruit glaze over the cake and scatter generously with coconut shavings. Serve cut into finger-width slices.

Per serving: 249 calories; 4g protein; 20g fat; 14g saturated fat; 14g carbohydrates; 8.7g sugar; 2.4g fiber; 0.1g sodium

white chocolate and orange scones

3 tablespoons unsalted butter, cut into
   small pieces, plus extra for greasing
1²/₃ cups self-rising flour
1 teaspoon baking powder
finely grated zest of 1 small orange
4 teaspoons Splenda granulated
   sweetener
3½ ounces white chocolate, chopped
   into very small pieces
   (about ½-²/₃ cups)
²/₃ cup low-fat milk, plus 1
   tablespoon for glazing

These sweet, orangey scones are best served freshly baked, but can also be frozen and warmed through when you serve them. For a summer version, try leaving out the white chocolate and serving them with strawberry jam and thick cream instead.

Preheat the oven to 425°F. Grease a baking sheet.

Put the flour and baking powder into a food processor. Add the butter and whizz until the mixture resembles fine breadcrumbs.

Add the orange zest and 3 teaspoons of the sweetener and blend briefly to combine. Add the chocolate and milk and blend again to make a soft dough.

Tip out onto a lightly floured counter and roll out to a ¾-inch thickness. Cut out circles using a 2-inch biscuit cutter and transfer to the baking sheet.

Mix the remaining sweetener with the tablespoon of milk and use to glaze the tops of the scones. Bake for about 10 minutes or until well risen and golden. Transfer to a wire rack to cool.

Per serving: 138 calories; 3g protein; 6g fat; 3.4g saturated fat; 20g carbohydrates; 5.9g sugar; 0.6g fiber; 0.13g sodium

pear crisp

SERVES 8

¾ cup (1½ sticks) unsalted butter, cut
   into cubes
6 Bosc pears, peeled, cored, and
   cubed
juice of 2 oranges
½ cup Splenda granulated sweetener
pinch of ground nutmeg
pinch of ground cinnamon
⅓ cup dry milk
½ cup ground almonds
¼ cup rolled oats (old-fashioned oats)
butter for greasing
⅔ cup dried coconut
1⅓ cups all-purpose flour
½ teaspoon salt
cup slivered almonds, toasted

This is the American equivalent of a British crumble. The oats, almonds, coconut, and spices make a lovely, crunchy topping.

Preheat the oven to 400°F. Grease the bottom of a deep baking dish with butter.

Combine the pears with the orange juice, 2 tablespoons of the sweetener, the nutmeg, and cinnamon, and place in the baking dish.

In a food processor, pulse together the dry milk, ground almonds, and rolled oats. Add the butter, coconut, flour, remaining sweetener, and salt, and continue to pulse until the mixture is crumbly. Fold in the toasted almonds.

Pop the mixture on top of the pears and bake in the oven for about 40 minutes, or until the top is golden. This dish is delicious served hot with thick cream.

Per serving: 618 calories; 7g protein; 51g fat; 28.3g saturated fat; 36g carbohydrates; 16.5g sugar; 5g fiber; 0.15g sodium

chocolate lovers

chocolate mousse cake

SERVES 6

3½ tablespoons unsalted butter, plus
  extra for greasing

¾ cup ready-to-eat pitted prunes,
  chopped

2 tablespoons Cointreau, Grand Marnier,
  or other orange liqueur

9 ounces (about 1½ cups) good-quality
  dark chocolate, broken into pieces

6 eggs, separated

4 tablespoons Splenda granulated
  sweetener

cocoa powder, for dusting

7 ounces (about 1½-1¾ cups)
  raspberries

This dense chocolatey cake is dotted with liqueur-steeped prunes which means there's no need to add lots of sugar. For the best result, cook until barely set in the center and serve warm with light cream so the flavors mingle together.

Preheat the oven to 325°F. Grease the bottom of an 8-inch springform pan or other cake pan with a removable bottom. Line with parchment paper (or foil).

Put the prunes and liqueur in the top of a double boiler with 1 tablespoon water and heat gently until bubbling around the edges. Remove from the heat.

Put the chocolate and butter in a heatproof bowl over a saucepan of barely simmering water and stir until melted. Alternatively, melt in the microwave for 1½ minutes at maximum power.

Whisk the egg yolks in a bowl with the sweetener for 2–3 minutes until slightly thickened. Using the clean beaters, beat the egg whites in a grease-free bowl until they hold their shape. Stir the melted chocolate mixture, the prunes, and any unabsorbed liqueur into the yolk mixture. Immediately fold in a third of the beaten egg whites using a large metal spoon, then fold in the rest.

Scoop into the pan, spreading the mixture gently to the edges. Bake for 18–20 minutes or until the cake has risen and forms a soft crust. The cake should still feel wobbly underneath when the pan is shaken.

Leave in the pan for 10 minutes, then carefully transfer to a serving plate. Dust with the cocoa powder and scatter the top with the raspberries.

Per serving: 471 calories; 11g protein; 33g fat; 16.2g saturated fat; 32g carbohydrates; 23.4g sugar; 4.7g fiber; 0.07g sodium

chocolate orange cheesecake

SERVES 8

for the graham cracker crust:
5 tablespoons (¾ stick) butter
1½ cups crushed graham crackers

for the filling:
1¾ tablespoons butter
4 ounces chocolate, broken into pieces
(about ⅔ cup)
1 tablespoon cocoa powder
2 tablespoons Cointreau or brandy
1 tablespoon granulated gelatin
(a scant cup)
7 ounces soft cheese (scant cup)
2 teaspoons finely grated orange zest
¼ cup Splenda granulated sweetener
2 eggs, separated

This lovely cheesecake is perfect for a special occasion. Make it the day before, then decorate shortly before serving.

For the graham cracker crust, melt the butter in a saucepan over a low heat. Stir in the crushed graham crackers. Tip into an 8-inch cake pan with a removable bottom or a pie plate and press into an even layer. Chill in the refrigerator until firm.

For the filling, put the butter, chocolate pieces, cocoa, and Cointreau or brandy into the top of a double boiler. Set it over simmering water and let it melt, stirring occasionally to blend. Cool slightly.

Put 5 tablespoons of just-boiled water into a small bowl. Sprinkle in the granulated gelatin, stirring to disperse it. Let dissolve for about 3 minutes, stirring from time to time, until the liquid is perfectly clear.

Beat the cream cheese in a large mixing bowl to soften it, then mix in the orange zest, sweetener, and egg yolks. Stir in the cooled chocolate mixture.

Beat the egg whites in a grease-free bowl until stiff. Use a large metal spoon to fold them into the chocolate mixture, then fold in the gelatin liquid. Pour over the graham cracker crust and chill until firm–this will take 2–3 hours.

Decorate the cheesecake to your liking. I've used whipped cream, chocolate curls, and shreds of orange zest.

Per serving: 497calories; 6g protein; 40g fat; 23g saturated fat; 28g carbohydrates; 17.1g sugar; 1g fiber; 0.29g sodium

pain au chocolat

MAKES 16

3 cups white bread flour

1 teaspoon salt

1 tablespoon Splenda granulated
   sweetener

¼-ounce (7g) envelope active dry yeast

¾ cup (1½ sticks) unsalted butter,
   softened

1 egg, beaten

flour, for dusting

2 egg yolks, beaten

6 ounces good-quality dark chocolate,
   broken into pieces (about a cup)

Nothing beats a homemade pain au chocolat!

Mix the flour, salt, sweetener, and yeast in a bowl. Melt 1 tablespoon of the butter and add to the bowl along with the beaten egg and a scant cup of warm water. Mix to a soft dough with a round-bladed knife. Turn out onto a floured surface and knead for 10 minutes until smooth and elastic.

Put the dough in a lightly oiled bowl and cover with plastic wrap. Let it rise in a warm place until doubled in size, about 1 hour. Roll the remaining butter between two sheets of waxed paper to a rectangle that measures roughly 12 x 3 inches. Chill until firm.

Punch the dough to deflate it and tip onto a lightly floured surface. Roll out to a rectangle that's slightly larger than the rectangle of butter, with a short end facing you. Peel the paper away from the butter and place the butter over the dough. Fold the bottom third of the dough up and the top third down to create a thick block of dough with three layers of butter inside. Give the dough a quarter turn and repeat the rolling and folding twice more, giving the dough a quarter turn each time. Chill for 15 minutes then roll, fold, and turn twice more. Chill again for 30 minutes.

Lightly grease two baking sheets. Mix the egg yolks with 1 teaspoon water. Roll out the dough on a lightly floured surface to a 14-inch square. (If the dough shrinks as you roll it, cover it and rest for 10 minutes.) Cut into 16 squares.

Press the chocolate pieces into the center of each square. Brush the edges of each square with egg yolk. Roll up into sausage shapes and space apart on the baking sheet. Cover with greased plastic wrap and let rise for 30–40 minutes until doubled in size. Preheat the oven to 400°F.

Brush the dough generously with egg yolk to glaze and bake for about 20 minutes until deep golden. Transfer to a wire rack to cool.

Per serving: 237 calories; 5g protein; 14g fat; 8g saturated fat; 24g carbohydrates; 3.5g sugar; 1.4g fiber; 0.13g sodium

sachertorte

SERVES 12

¾ cup (1½ sticks) unsalted butter,
  softened, plus extra for greasing
9 ounces good-quality dark chocolate,
  broken into pieces (about 1½ cups)
⅓ cup brandy or almond liqueur
⅓ cup Splenda granulated sweetener
5 eggs, separated
a scant cup self-rising flour
1 cup ground almonds

for the glaze:
¼ cup apricot jam
  (see recipe page 80)
1 tablespoon brandy or almond liqueur
⅔ cup heavy cream
3½ ounces good-quality dark chocolate,
  chopped (about ½-⅔ cup)
1 ounce milk chocolate, chopped
  (about 2-3 tablespoons)

A traditional Austrian Sachertorte is densely rich and smothered in a dark, glossy chocolate syrup with "Sacher" piped on top. This simplified version is equally rich and delicious but uses a chocolate cream glaze. Store the cake in a cool place rather than the fridge for the best result.

Preheat the oven to 325°F. Grease the bottom and sides of an 8-inch round cake pan. Line with parchment paper and grease the paper. Put the dark chocolate and liqueur into the top of a double boiler and place over barely simmering water. Let it melt, stirring frequently. Alternatively, melt in the microwave for 1½ minutes at maximum power.

Beat the butter and sweetener with a hand-held electric beater until pale and creamy. Stir in the melted chocolate, then the egg yolks, flour, and almonds.

Using clean beaters, beat the egg whites in a grease-free bowl until stiff. Fold a quarter of the egg whites into the chocolate mixture with a large metal spoon, then fold in the rest.

Turn into the pan and level the surface. Bake for 30–35 minutes or until a skewer, inserted into the center, comes out clean. Leave in the pan for 10 minutes then transfer to a wire rack to cool completely.

To make the glaze, press the apricot jam through a fine mesh strainer into a small bowl and stir in the liqueur. Pour onto the cake and brush it all over. Put the cream and dark chocolate in the top of a double boiler and set it over a saucepan of barely simmering water. Stir until melted. Melt the milk chocolate in the same way, or microwave on medium power for 1 minute.

Pour the dark chocolate mixture over the top of the cake and spread to the edges and down the sides with an icing spatula or butter knife. Using a teaspoon, dribble lines of milk chocolate over the top of the cake to decorate it.

Per serving: 505 calories; 8g protein; 38g fat; 18.8g saturated fat; 29g carbohydrates; 16.2g sugar; 2.6g fiber; 0.08g sodium

chocolate brownies

MAKES 15

9 ounces dark chocolate, chopped
   (about 1½ cups)

¾ cup (1½ sticks) unsalted butter

3 eggs

1 ounce Splenda granulated sweetener

½ cup all-purpose flour

1 teaspoon baking powder

1 cup walnuts, roughly chopped

Melinda says: Everyone loves chocolate brownies! I make these for the family all the time and treat my kids to them after school—they don't stay on the plate for long!

Preheat the oven to 375°F. Grease and line a shallow 8 x 10-inch baking pan and lightly dust with flour.

Put the chocolate and butter in a double boiler and set it over gently simmering water. Let it melt, stirring frequently. Alternatively melt in the microwave for 2 minutes at maximum power.

Beat the eggs in a bowl, gradually beating in the sweetener until combined. Beat in the melted chocolate mixture. Sift the flour and baking powder into the bowl. Add the walnuts and stir the ingredients together until just combined.

Turn into the pan and spread the mixture into the corners. Bake for about 15 minutes or until the surface is set but the mixture feels very soft underneath. Let it cool in the pan. Cut into squares and store in an airtight tin.

Per serving: 252 calories; 3g protein; 20g fat; 9.5g saturated fat; 16g carbohydrates; 12.3g sugar; 0.8g fiber; 0.07g sodium

chocolate cherry sundaes

SERVES 4

1 cup fresh cherries

2 tablespoons Splenda granulated
sweetener

1 teaspoon cornstarch, blended with 1
tablespoon cold water

3-ounce container lowfat cream cheese

2 tablespoons lowfat milk

½ teaspoon vanilla extract

for the chocolate sauce:

2 ounces dark chocolate, broken into
pieces (about ¼-¹/₃ cup)

2 teaspoons cocoa powder

1 teaspoon cornstarch, blended with 1
tablespoon cold water

2 tablespoons golden syrup or cornsyrup

**If you've ever eaten Black Forest gâteau, you'll know how good the
combination of cherries and chocolate is, so try them together again in
this fabulous dessert.**

Reserve 4 cherries for decoration, then cut in half and pit the rest. Put them
into a small saucepan with ²/₃ cup water and 1 tablespoon of the sweetener.
Simmer for 3–4 minutes, until softened. Stir in the blended cornstarch and
cook, while stirring, until thickened. Remove from the heat and l et cool, stirring
occasionally to prevent a skin from forming.

Meanwhile, beat together the lowfat cream cheese, milk, vanilla extract, and
remaining sweetener until smooth.

Make the chocolate sauce by putting the chocolate, cocoa powder, blended
cornstarch, and golden syrup into a small saucepan. Heat, stirring constantly,
until smooth and blended. Cool for a few minutes, stirring to prevent a skin
from forming.

Spoon the cherries, chocolate sauce, and cream cheese mixture into layers in
pretty serving glasses. Pop a fresh cherry on top of each one, then chill until
ready to serve.

Per serving: 160 calories; 4g protein; 5g fat; 3g saturated fat; 25g carbohydrates;
21.9g sugar; 1g fiber; 0.13g sodium

chocolate ice cream

SERVES 6

5 egg yolks

3 tablespoons Splenda granulated
   sweetener

2 cups milk

5½ ounces good-quality milk
   chocolate,
   broken into small pieces

1 cup heavy cream

It is thought that as far back as 200BC, the Chinese ate some version of ice cream, and that the Roman Emperor Nero is said to have had a passion for it. The best ice cream for me is a homemade, custard-based chocolate ice cream—made with good quality chocolate.

Whisk the egg yolks with the sweetener in a bowl until light and frothy. In a small pan, heat the milk, bringing it to boiling point for just a couple of seconds. Remove from the heat and pour the hot milk into the egg yolk mixture, stirring all the time. Then pour the whole lot back into the saucepan and gently reheat, stirring constantly, until the custard is thickened. Don't allow the custard to boil or it will curdle!

Once thickened, drop in the chocolate pieces. Stir until the chocolate is melted and well combined with the custard. Remove from the heat and allow the mixture to cool. Chill in the freezer for a couple of hours until slushy.

Whip the double cream until you have soft peaks. Mix this into the chocolate and transfer to an ice-cream machine. Churn according to the instructions. Eat and enjoy!

Per serving: 440kcal; 8g protein; 38g fat; 19.9g saturated fat; 17g carbohydrates; 12.4g sugar; 1.5g fibre; 0.06g sodium

simple chocolate soufflé

SERVES 4

butter, for greasing
¼ cup finely chopped nuts
2 teaspoons cocoa powder
¼ cup cornstarch
1 cup milk
4 ounces dark chocolate (minimum 70% cocoa solids), broken into pieces (about ¾ cup)
1 tablespoon freeze-dried instant coffee
5 tablespoons Splenda granulated sweetener, plus 1 teaspoon
3 egg yolks
5 egg whites

Don't be scared of the old soufflé. As long as you follow the rules and stick to the recipe, it'll work, I promise. Remember to have your guests ready and waiting at the table so you can bring the soufflé right from the oven to the table. You can make the souffle either in a large dish or in individual dishes.

Preheat the oven to 375°F. Liberally butter a 1.5 quart soufflé dish and sprinkle the butter with the finely chopped nuts and cocoa powder.

Mix the cornstarch with a little of the milk to a smooth paste.

Heat the remaining milk with the dark chocolate and coffee granules in a saucepan. Add the 5 tablespoons sweetener and stir until the chocolate has completely melted.

Pour in the cornstarch paste and boil for 1 minute until thickened. Remove from the heat and stir in the egg yolks, one by one. Let it cool a little while you beat the egg whites in a grease-free bowl until stiff. Fold the egg whites and the remaining sweetener into the chocolate mixture.

Pour into the prepared soufflé dish and cook for 35 minutes. Serve immediately.

Per serving: 406 calories; 12g protein; 27g fat; 9.5g saturated fat; 30g carbohydrates; 17.8g sugar; 2.9g fiber; 0.13g sodium

cherry, apricot, and chocolate chip oatbars

MAKES 16

¾ cup (1½ sticks) butter, plus extra for greasing

½ golden syrup (if unavailable, use corn syrup)

¼ cup Splenda granulated sweetener

3 cups rolled oats (old-fashioned oats)

pinch of salt

⅓ cup dried cherries, cut in half

½ cup ready-to-eat dried apricots, chopped

¼ cup white chocolate chips

¼ cup dark or milk chocolate chips

The dried cherries and chocolate chips give these oatbars a delicious new twist!

Preheat the oven to 350°F. Grease an 8-inch square baking pan and line it with parchment paper–by leaving an overhang of paper, the oatbars will be easier to remove later.

Melt the butter with the golden syrup in a large saucepan over a gentle heat. Bring to a boil and cook for 2 minutes, stirring constantly. Remove from the heat.

Mix together the sweetener, oats, salt, cherries, apricots, and chocolate chips. Add to the saucepan and stir together until thoroughly mixed. Tip into the prepared pan and level the surface with the back of a spoon.

Bake for 20–25 minutes until golden brown. Cool for 30 minutes, then remove from the pan and cut into 16 squares. Let cool completely on a wire rack. Keep in an airtight container.

Per serving: 229 calories; 4g protein; 12g fat; 6.8g saturated fat; 29g carbohydrates; 16.2g sugar; 2.4g fiber; 0.15g sodium

cakes and muffins

carrot cake muffins

MAKES 12

2¾ cups wholwheat flour
2½ teaspoons baking powder
1¼ teaspoons apple pie spice
½ teaspoon salt
²/₃ cup ground almonds
1 extra large egg, beaten
1¼ teaspoons vanilla extract
½ cup vegetable oil
½ cup lowfat milk
¾ cup plus 2 tablespoons Splenda
    granulated sweetener
finely grated zest of 1 orange
15 ounces carrots, peeled and finely
    grated (about 3 cups)
heaping ¹/₃ cup raisins

for the frosting:
¾ cup light soft cream cheese
1 tablespoon Splenda granulated
    sweetener

If you love carrot cake, then you'll adore these muffins...

Preheat the oven to 400°F. Place twelve paper muffin cups into a muffin pan, or grease the cups in the muffin pan.

Sift the flour, baking powder, apple pie spice, and salt into a large mixing bowl. (Add any bran bits left in the sifter from the wholewheat flour back into the bowl.) Stir in the ground almonds.

Beat together the egg, vanilla extract, vegetable oil, milk, sweetener, and most of the orange zest. Add the grated carrots and stir well.

Tip the wet ingredients and raisins into the bowl of dry ingredients. Stir until just combined. Avoid over-mixing and do not beat. Spoon the mixture into the muffin cups. Transfer to the oven and bake for 20–25 minutes until risen and golden. Cool on a wire rack.

To make the frosting, mix together the cream cheese and sweetener until smooth. Top the muffins with the frosting and sprinkle them with the reserved orange zest.

Per serving: 288 calories; 7g protein; 14g fat; 2.2g saturated fat; 35g carbohydrates; 11.4g sugar; 2.4g fiber; 0.31g sodium

fresh strawberry sponge cake

SERVES 8

3 tablespoons unsalted butter, melted,
   plus extra for greasing
2 tablespoons caster sugar
4 tablespoons Splenda granulated
   sweetener
5 eggs
¾ cup all-purpose flour

for the topping:
14 ounces strawberries, hulled
   (about 3½–4 cups)
1 tablespoon Splenda granulated
   sweetener
scant cup heavy cream

This cake is made with a génoise cake batter—a light and airy whisked batter—with the addition of melted butter that adds extra flavor and moisture, and makes it keep slightly longer. It's delicious served as it is here, in a single layer with whipped cream and fresh strawberries, or you can sandwich the cream and fruit between two cake layers.

Preheat the oven to 350°F. Grease the insides of two 8-inch cake pans with removable bottoms. Line the bottoms with kitchen parchment.

Put the sugar, sweetener, and eggs in the top of a double boiler over barely simmering water and beat with a hand-held electric beater until the beaters leave a trail when lifted from the pan. Remove from the heat and beat for a further 2 minutes.

Pour the melted butter around the edges of the mixture. Sift half the flour into the pan and fold in with the butter, using a large metal spoon. Sift the remaining flour into the pan and fold in. Divide between the cake pans and spread gently to the edges.

Bake for 18–20 minutes until pale golden around the edges and just firm to the touch. Unhinge the edges and transfer the cakes to a wire rack to cool. Meanwhile, make a sauce by blitzing half the strawberries with the Splenda in a food processor. Strainer through a fine mesh strainer into a little bowl. Slice the remaining strawberries.

Beat the cream until it forms soft peaks. Spread it over the cake, and top with the sliced strawberries and the sauce.

Per serving: 284 calories; 6g protein; 22g fat; 11.4g saturated fat; 17g carbohydrates; 7.8g sugar; 0.9g fiber; 0.05g sodium

ricotta cake

vegetable oil, for greasing

1 cup plus 2 tablespoons unsalted
   butter, softened

½ cup sugar

¼ cup Splenda granulated
   sweetener

8 eggs, separated

finely grated zest of 2 oranges

finely grated zest of 3 lemons

7 ounces mixed dried fruits
   (about 1¼-1½ cups)

²/₃ cup roasted hazelnuts, roughly
   chopped

9 ounces ricotta cheese (about 1 cup)

²/₃ cup flour

This cake is good for even the most hopeless of cooks. I've used whole cranberries, cherries, and blueberries, and chopped apricots, but you can mix and match what you have in the cupboard or what appeals to you when out shopping. Equally you can use different nuts, too.

Preheat the oven to 350°F. Grease a 9 x 2-inch springform cake pan sparingly with vegetable oil.

Cream the butter, sugar, and sweetener together until pale and fluffy. Add the egg yolks one by one, beating well between each addition.

In a separate bowl, fold the citrus zest, dried fruits, and nuts into the ricotta. Fold in the butter and egg mixture. Sift the flour into this mix, and combine.

Using clean beaters, beat the egg whites to soft peaks. Mix 1 tablespoon of the egg whites into the ricotta batter. Once this is amalgamated, fold in the rest carefully, ensuring that you do not lose too much of the air.

Pour the mixture into the prepared cake pan and bake for 50 minutes. The rule about inserting the tip of a knife into the center and coming out clean does not apply to this cake as it is very moist. The best way to tell if it is cooked is to shake the pan gently; if the cake wobbles very slightly, it needs just a little while longer to finish cooking.

Per serving: 397 calories; 8g protein; 28g fat; 13.8g saturated fat; 29g carbohydrates; 22.8g sugar; 1.5g fiber; 0.07g sodium

apple, apricot and sultana crumble cake

SERVES 8

$2/3$ cup minus 2 teaspoons Splenda
  granulated sweetener

1½ rolled oats (old-fashioned oats)

1 cup muesli (or granola)

1 teaspoon apple pie spice

$2/3$ cup (1¼ sticks) butter, melted

1 egg, beaten

2 eating apples, peeled, cored,
  and sliced

1 tablespoon fresh lemon juice

$2/3$ cup ready-to-eat dried apricots,
  chopped

$1/3$ cup golden raisins

plain yogurt, light cream, or ice
  cream, for serving

You'll love this delicious cake—it's great for a snack or as a dessert.

Preheat the oven to 350°F. Grease and line an 8-inch round cake pan with a removable bottom. Line the bottom with kitchen parchment.

Mix together the sweetener, oats, muesli, and apple pie spice. Stir in the melted butter, then mix in the beaten egg. In a separate bowl, mix together the apple slices, lemon juice, apricots, and raisins.

Tip about two thirds of the oat mixture into the prepared cake pan. Press down lightly and arrange half the fruit mixture on top. Sprinkle with the remaining oat mixture and level the surface. Top with the remaining fruit, pressing it down lightly again.

Bake for 35–40 minutes until firm and golden brown. Place the cake pan on a wire rack and let cool for 15–20 minutes. Carefully unhinge the sides and remove the cake from the pan. If using, peel away the paper lining. Serve warm or cold with yogurt, cream, or ice cream.

Per serving: 324 calories; 6g protein; 18g fat; 10.4g saturated fat; 36g carbohydrates; 17.3g sugar; 4.3g fiber; 0.18g sodium

bakewell tarts

SERVES 8

12 ounces puff pastry, thawed if frozen
flour, for dusting
8 teaspoons raspberry or strawberry jam
5 tablespoons (¾ stick) butter, softened
⅓ cup plus 2 teaspoons Splenda
  granulated sweetener
1 egg, beaten
1 cup ground almonds

Puff pastry gives a lovely lift to these melt-in-the-mouth almond tarts. They're lovely served with custard or light cream.

Preheat the oven to 400°F.

Roll out the pastry on a lightly floured work surface. Use a 10cm fluted cutter to stamp out 8 rounds, then use them to line 8 Yorkshire pudding tins or individual tart tins. Prick the bases with a fork. Place 1 teaspoon of jam into each one, spreading it over the middle of the pastry. Stand the tins on a baking tray.

Beat together the butter, sweetener, beaten egg, and ground almonds. Share this mixture between the tarts, spreading it out to cover the jam.

Bake for 20–25 minutes, until the pastry is risen and golden brown. Leave them to cool for a few minutes before serving.

Per serving: 336kcal; 6g protein; 26g fat; 9.7g saturated fat; 22g carbohydrates; 5.7g sugar; 0.9g fibre; 0.2g sodium

moist cherry cake

SERVES 8

1 cup plus 2 tablespoons unsalted butter, softened, plus extra for greasing

12 ounces (about 1½ cups) fresh cherries

½ cup Splenda granulated sweetener

5 eggs, separated

1 teaspoon almond extract

1½ ground almonds

¾ cup self-rising flour

Melinda says: This recipe gives you the chance to make the most of fresh cherries during their season. I really like making this cake at the weekend with help from my daughter—and I always catch her licking the spoon...

Preheat the oven to 350°F. Grease the bottom and sides of an 8-inch springform pan. Line with parchment paper and grease the parchment. Cut the cherries in half and remove the pits.

Using a hand-held electric beater, beat together the butter and all but 2 tablespoons of the sweetener until pale, creamy, and very soft. Beat in the egg yolks, almond extract, ground almonds, flour and 1 tablespoon warm water.

Whisk the egg whites in a thoroughly clean bowl until they form soft peaks, then whisk in the remaining sweetener. Using a large metal spoon, gently fold a quarter of the egg whites into the almond mixture. Gently fold in the rest, along with half the cherries.

Turn the mixture into the pan and spread it out in an even layer. Scatter the remaining cherries on top. Bake for about 50 minutes until the cake is risen and firm to the touch. Test by piercing the center of the cake with a skewer—it should come out fairly clean. Let it cool in the pan, then transfer to a serving plate. The cake can be stored for a couple of days without drying out.

Per serving: 460 calories; 9g protein; 40g fat; 18g saturated fat; 17g carbohydrates; 7.3g sugar; 2.1g fiber; 0.09g sodium

apple and cinnamon muffins

MAKES 18

vegetable oil or butter, for greasing

2 tart apples, peeled, cored,
  and chopped

¼ cup plus 1 tablespoon Splenda
  granulated sweetener

½ cup (1 stick) unsalted butter

1 teaspoon fresh lemon juice

¾ cup plus 2 tablespoons plain flour

pinch of salt

1 tablespoon baking powder

1 tablespoon baking soda

1 teaspoon ground cinnamon

2 eggs, lightly beaten

¾ cup milk

¾ cup golden syrup (if unavailable use
  corn syrup)

The combination of apples and cinnamon is a classic one—here the cinnamon makes the body of the muffins extra rich and interesting.

Preheat the oven to 350°F. Grease the muffin pan with vegetable oil or butter.

In a small saucepan, cook the apples, together with 4 tablespoons of the sweetener, 2 tablespoons of the butter, and the lemon juice until the apples are soft but not mushy and the liquid has almost evaporated. Set aside to cool.

Sift the flour, salt, baking powder, baking soda, and cinnamon into a bowl. Stir in the remaining sweetener.

Melt the remaining butter, then add the eggs, milk, and golden syrup. Gently stir in the apple mixture.

Pour the wet mixture into the dry ingredients and stir just enough to bind them. The batter should not be smooth. Spoon into the prepared muffin pan(s) so each cup is about two-thirds full. Bake for about 20 minutes or until a skewer pushed into the center comes out clean. Cool on a wire rack.

Per serving: 141 calories; 2g protein; 6g fat; 3.5g saturated fat; 21g carbohydrates; 15.5g sugar; 0.4g fiber; 0.44g sodium

blueberry muffins

MAKES 12

¼ cup vegetable oil, plus extra
  for greasing
1½ cups flour
2 teaspoons baking powder
3 tablespoons Splenda granulated
  sweetener
¾ cup milk or buttermilk
1 egg
7 ounces blueberries, (about 1½ cups)

You could use chocolate chips in place of the blueberries if you like.

Preheat the oven to 350°F. Thoroughly grease a 12-cup muffin pan with vegetable oil. This is best done in advance so that the batter doesn't have to wait before being poured into the cups.

Sift the flour and baking powder into a large mixing bowl, and gently stir in the sweetener.

In a separate bowl, mix the milk, egg, and the ¼ cup of oil together. Make a well in the center of the flour and slowly mix in the liquid. When all the liquid is added, beat well, and add the blueberries.

Spoon the mixture into the prepared muffin pan so each cup is about two-thirds full. Bake in the oven for 20–25 minutes. You can test whether the muffins are ready by pressing lightly on one; if the top springs back, they are done.

Cool the muffins on a wire rack. You can eat them on their own, but I think they are best when served slightly warm, split, and spread with butter and jam.

Per serving: 129 calories; 3g protein; 5g fat; 0.8g saturated fat; 19g carbohydrates; 6.1g sugar; 0.8g fiber; 0.11g sodium

raspberry and banana muffins

MAKES 12

2¹/₃ cups flour

1 tablespoon baking powder

¾ cup Splenda granulated sweetener

5 ounces frozen raspberries
  (about 1¼-1¾), briefly thawed

1 large egg

1½ teaspoons vanilla extract

5 tablespoons (¾ stick) butter, melted

²/₃ cup lowfat milk

1½ (or 2 small) ripe bananas,
  mashed

I've used frozen raspberries in this recipe as they tend to have a more intense flavor than fresh ones.

Preheat the oven to 400°F. Place 12 paper muffin cups into a muffin pan.

Sift the flour and baking powder into a large mixing bowl. Stir in the sweetener and raspberries.

Beat together the egg, vanilla extract, melted butter, and milk. Stir into the dry ingredients along with the mashed banana until just combined. Avoid overmixing and do not beat. The mixture will be quite lumpy, but there should not be any traces of dry flour. Spoon into the paper cups.

Bake for 20–25 minutes until risen and golden. Cool on a wire rack.

Per serving: 171 calories; 4g protein; 6g fat; 3.6g saturated fat; 26g carbohydrates; 6g sugar; 1.2g fiber; 0.2g sodium

porter cake

SERVES 8

¾ cup (1½ sticks) unsalted butter,
   cut into cubes, plus extra for greasing
18 ounces mixed dried fruit
   (about 3-3½ cups)
finely grated zest of 1 lemon
½ cup Splenda granulated sweetener
1 tablespoon black treacle or molasses
scant cup porter or stout
1 teaspoon baking soda
3 eggs, beaten
9 ounces flour (1¾-2 cups)
1 tablespoon apple pie spice

Porter, a dark, richly flavored beer, similar to a stout such as Guinness, adds a great flavor to rich fruitcakes. This simple fruitcake is so easy to make and keeps very well for up to a week, if it hangs around that long!

Preheat the oven to 300°F. Grease the bottom and sides of an 8-inch round cake pan and line with parchment paper or foil, shiny side up. Grease the paper (or foil) too.

Put the butter, dried fruit, lemon zest, sweetener, treacle, and porter or stout in a large saucepan. Bring to a boil and stir frequently until the butter has dissolved. Reduce the heat and simmer gently for 10 minutes until the juices are thickened and syrupy. Let cool for 10 minutes.

Stir in the baking soda so the mixture becomes foamy, then stir in the beaten eggs. Sift in the flour and spice and mix until combined. Spoon into the pan and level the surface.

Bake for about 1 hour or until a skewer, inserted into the center, comes out clean. Let cool in the pan. Store in an airtight container.

Per serving: 489 calories; 7g protein; 21g fat; 12.1g saturated fat; 71g carbohydrates; 46.5g sugar; 2.5g fiber; 0.24g sodium

angel food cake

SERVES 8

2 teaspoons vegetable oil

½ cup flour, plus extra for dusting

¼ cup sugar

2/3 cup minus 2 teaspoons Splenda
  granulated sweetener

8 egg whites

1 teaspoon cream of tartar

2/3 cup dry nonfat milk

1 teaspoon vanilla extract

pulp of 2 passionfruit

a handful of raspberries

for the frosting:

9 ounces mascarpone cheese
  (about 1 cup)

1¼ cups heavy cream

2 tablespoons Limoncello or other citrus
  liqueur

2 tablespoons lemon juice

1 teaspoon Splenda granulated
  sweetener

This sweet, vanilla-scented sponge cake can be made using a decorative kugelhopf pan or a plain tube pan—as long as there's a hole in the center to allow for quick, even cooking. Angel food cake can be served just as it is, but for this recipe I've done something a little more special—I've smothered it in a liqueur and mascarpone frosting which completes its whiter than white appeal.

Preheat the oven to 325°F. Brush a 1½-quart kugelhopf or plain tube pan with the oil and coat with flour, tapping out the excess. Mix together the sugar and sweetener and set aside.

Beat the egg whites in a thoroughly clean bowl until foamy. Add the cream of tartar and beat again until stiff. Gradually beat in the sugar and sweetener, a spoonful at a time. Stir in the dry milk and vanilla extract. Sift a thin layer of flour over the batter and fold in using a large metal spoon. Continue to sift and fold in the rest of the flour.

Turn the batter into the pan and level the surface. Bake for 20–25 minutes until firm to the touch. Loosen around the edges of the pan with a knife and invert onto a wire rack but leave the pan in position over the cake while the cake cools. (If the cake has risen too high above the top of the pan, cut a little off but bear in mind that the cake will shrink back as it cools.) Once cool, transfer to a plate.

To make the frosting, beat the mascarpone in a bowl until softened. Add the cream, liqueur, lemon juice ,and sweetener, and beat until smooth. Using a pastry spatula or butter knife, spread the cream mixture over the cake, swirling it decoratively with the tip of the knife. Scatter the fruits over the top of the cake to finish.

Per serving: 455 calories; 8g protein; 36g fat; 20.5g saturated fat; 25g carbohydrates; 16.9g sugar; 0.9g fiber; 0.35g sodium

CAKES AND MUFFINS

fig streusel

SERVES 8

scant cup red wine

2 teaspoons Splenda granulated
   sweetener

1 ounce fresh ginger, peeled and grated
   (about 2 tablespoons)

8 fresh figs, quartered

7 ounces red grapes, cut in half
   (about 1⅓ cups)

1½ teaspoons cornstarch

for the streusel:

1½ cups flour

1 teaspoon apple pie spice

¾ cup (1½ sticks) lightly salted butter,
   cut into small cubes

½ cup Splenda granulated
   sweetener

¾ cup ground almonds

1 egg

2 tablespoons slivered almonds, lightly
   toasted

Streusels are great for serving with a cup of coffee or, when freshly baked, as a dessert with spoonfuls of whipped cream or crème fraîche. The red wine and ginger give the cake a warm, wintry flavor.

Preheat the oven to 350°F. Grease the insides of a 9-inch springform pan (or other 9-inch cake pan with a removable bottom).

Put the wine in a saucepan with the sweetener and ginger and bring slowly to a boil. Reduce the heat to a gentle simmer and add the figs and grapes. Turn the fruits gently in the syrup for 1 minute, then remove with a slotted spoon and place in a bowl.

Blend the cornstarch with 1 tablespoon water and add to the pan. Bring to a boil, stirring until thickened. Pour this over the fruits and stir gently to mix. Let cool while you make the streusel.

Put the flour and apple pie spice in a food processor along with the butter. Blend until the mixture resembles fine breadcrumbs. Add the sweetener and ground almonds and blend again until the mixture forms a coarse crumble. Measure out ¾ cup of the crumble mixture and set aside. Add the egg to the remaining mixture and blend to a paste.

Tip the paste into the pan and press down over the bottom and slightly up the sides as you would for a graham cracker crust. Bake for 15 minutes.

Scatter the fig mixture and juices over the pie crust, piling them up slightly in the center. Sprinkle the crumble mixture on top and scatter the almonds over that. Bake for 30 minutes until pale golden. Let cool slightly in the pan, then serve warm or cold.

Per serving: 396 calories; 7g protein; 26g fat; 12.1g saturated fat; 34g carbohydrates; 13.7g sugar; 2.6g fiber; 0.15g sodium

jams, spreads, and sauces

lemon curd

MAKES ABOUT 1-1½ CUPS

zest and juice of 4 large unwaxed
    lemons
2 organic eggs, plus 2 egg yolks
²/₃ cup (1¼ sticks) unsalted butter, cut into
    small cubes
¹/₃ cup Splenda granulated
    sweetener

A fresh, zesty lemon curd is perfect for spreading over warm toast or as a filling for a sponge cake. For a good, rich color, make sure you use organic eggs.

Place all the ingredients in the top of a double boiler set over gently simmering water. (Make sure the bottom of the top pan is not touching the water or the mixture will overheat.)

Cook the mixture gently, stirring frequently with a wooden spoon until the butter and sweetener have dissolved. Continue to cook, stirring constantly, until the lemon curd is thickened enough to thinly coat the back of the wooden spoon. This will take about 15 minutes.

Strain through a strainer into sterilized jars (see below) and let cool. Cover with wax paper and screw on the lids and let cool. Store in the fridge—the lemon curd will keep for up to three weeks.

Per 1½ tablespoon serving: 96 calories; 1g protein; 10g fat; 5.6g saturated fat; 1g carbohydrates; 0.8g sugar; 0g fiber; 0.01g sodium

how to sterilize jars

To sterilize jars, wash the jars thoroughly in warm, soapy water, scrubbing off any old labels. Preheat the oven to 300°F. Put the jars on a wire rack set inside a baking tray and heat in the oven for 15 minutes. Alternatively, scrub any old labels off the jars and then run the upturned jars through a hot dishwasher cycle.

cranberry sauce

SERVES 6

¼ cup Splenda granulated sweetener
1 pound, 10 ounces fresh or frozen
   cranberries (about 8-8½ cups)
pinch of ground cinnamon
pinch of grated nutmeg
raisins, currants, or orange peel
   (optional)

Cranberry sauce is an essential accompaniment to turkey at any Thanksgiving dinner, and here's a low-calorie version.

Put the sweetener and 1 cup of water into a heavy saucepan and heat gently to dissolve the sweetener. Add the cranberries, bring to a boil, and cook for 10 minutes until the berries burst.

Stir in the spices and, if using, any of the optional ingredients. Remove from the heat and let cool completely, then chill in the fridge.

Per serving: 25 calories; 1g protein; 0g fat; 0g saturated fat; 5g carbohydrates; 5.2g sugar; 3.8g fiber; 0g sodium

homemade chocolate-nut spread

MAKES ABOUT 1 POUND

9 ounces whole hazelnuts (about 2 cups)
3 tablespoons Splenda granulated
  sweetener
¼ cup (unsweetened) cocoa
  powder
½ teaspoon vanilla extract
about ¼ cup vegetable oil

When you really need a chocolate fix and there isn't a jar of Nutella at hand, this simple spread will do the trick. It's fun to make for the kids, too. It can be stored in an airtight jar for up to one month.

Preheat the oven to 350°F.

Spread the hazelnuts on a tray and toast them in the oven until the skins are blackened, turning them once–this will take about 15 minutes. Remove from the oven and let cool until you can handle them. Remove the bitter skins by putting the nuts into a paper bag and rubbing until most of the skins have come off. It doesn't matter if there are still specs of blackened skin on the nuts as long as you get rid of most of the skins.

Put the hazelnuts into a blender and blitz–the nuts get crushed first, then become a fine powder, and finally form a ball around the blade, making hazelnut butter. This will take about 5 minutes.

Add the sweetener, cocoa powder, and vanilla extract and, with the blender on a low speed, drizzle in enough oil to make the right consistency of chocolate spread.

Spoon the mixture into a clean airtight glass jar and store in the fridge. Stir the chocolate spread before using it, as it will solidify a little when chilled.

Per 25g serving: 121 calories; 2g protein; 12g fat; 1.1g saturated fat; 2g carbohydrates; 1g sugar; 1.1g fiber; 0g sodium

apricot jam

MAKES ABOUT 1¼ POUNDS

1½ teaspoons granulated gelatin

18 ounces pitted fresh apricots, roughly
    chopped (about 2½-3 cups)

1 cup apple juice

1 tablespoon fresh lemon juice

½ cup Splenda granulated
    sweetener

This delicious, tangy fruit spread technically isn't a jam—without sugar used in the method, it doesn't have the same preservative qualities a true jam would have. It's therefore best made in small quantities and it keeps in the fridge for up to three weeks.

Put 2 tablespoons water into a bowl and stir in the gelatin. Let it soak while you cook the apricots.

Put the apricots into a saucepan and pour in the apple and lemon juice. Bring to a boil, turn down the heat, and simmer gently, uncovered, for about 10 minutes or until the apricots are soft. Skim off any foam that collects on the surface using a slotted spoon.

Remove the pan from the heat and stir in the sweetener. Add the gelatin mixture and stir again until dissolved. Ladle into sterilized jars (see page 76), and cover with discs of wax paper and then the lids while still hot.

Per 1½ tablespoons serving: 12k calories; 0g protein; 0g fat; 0g saturated fat; 3g carbohydrates; 2.7g sugar; 0.3g fiber; 0g sodium

mango and passionfruit sauce

SERVES 4

1 ripe mango, peeled and pitted

2 passionfruit, cut in half

2 tablespoons Splenda granulated
   sweetener

Cut the mango into chunks and scoop the flesh out of the passionfruit. Place the fruits in a food processor along with the sweetener and whizz until you have a smooth puree. Scoop the purée into a fine mesh strainer and push through into a nice bowl or sauceboat.

The sauce can be stirred into yogurt, poured over a scoop of good ice cream, or served with a fruit-filled crêpe.

Per serving: 44 calories; 1g protein; 0g fat; 0g saturated fat; 11g carbohydrates; 10.5g sugar; 2g fiber; 0g sodium

blood orange curd

MAKES ABOUT 1½ CUPS

½ cup blood orange juice

1 tablespoon finely grated blood orange
   zest

½ cup (1 stick) unsalted butter

1½ tablespoons Splenda granulated
   sweetener

3 eggs plus 1 egg yolk

Blood oranges are a wonderful alternative to lemon in this recipe.

Put the orange juice, orange zest, butter, and sweetener into a small pan and place over a gentle heat. Stir until the butter is melted and everything is mixed together thoroughly.

Remove the pan from the heat and slowly whisk in the eggs, one at a time, until the mixture thickens–this will take a few minutes. Finally, whisk in the egg yolk.

Cool the mixture and put into sterilized, airtight jars (see page 76). It will keep in the fridge for a couple of weeks. This curd is great on toast, as a filling for a tart, or, for a change, sandwiched between two layers of Victoria sponge cake.

Per 1½ tablespoons: 84 calories; 2g protein; 8g fat; 4.7g saturated fat; 1g carbohydrates; 0.8g sugar; 0g fiber; 0.02g sodium

blackberry relish

MAKES ABOUT 3¼ POUNDS

2 pounds blackberries (about 7 cups)

2–3 tablespoons Splenda granulated
sweetener

5 tablespoons apple juice

2 teaspoons allspice

2 tablespoons ground ginger

2 cups white vinegar

We've been making relishes for years. This blackberry relish is a nice combo with a strong, sharp cheddar cheese or with cold meats.

In a bowl, toss the blackberries gently in the sweetener, apple juice, and the two spices and let rest overnight for the flavors to mingle.

Bring the vinegar to a boil, add the berries, reduce the heat, and cook gently for 20 minutes. Let cool and spoon into sterilized jars (see page 76). The relish keeps in the fridge for one month.

Per 1½ tablespoons: 18 calories; 0g protein; 0g fat; 0g saturated fat; 4g carbohydrates; 4g sugar; 0.5g fiber; 0g sodium

blackberry chutney

MAKES ABOUT 4 POUNDS

3 pounds blackberries (about 10-11 cups)

1 pounds apples, peeled, cored, and
chopped (about 3 cups)

8 ounces onions, finely chopped
(about 2 cups)

1 teaspoon ground ginger

1 teaspoon English mustard powder

¼ teaspoon grated nutmeg

¼ teaspoon ground mace

²/₃ cup minus 2 teapoons Splenda
granulated sweetener

¹/₃ cup apple juice

2½ cups white vinegar

sea salt (or kosher salt)
and crushed black pepper

Place all the ingredients into a large, heavy pot with 1 teaspoon salt and 1 teaspoon pepper. Bring to a boil, turn down the heat, and simmer for about 1 hour until it's the thickness you want, remembering that it will be a little thicker when cold.

Spoon into hot, sterilized jars (see page 76) and seal. Once cooled, store in the fridge. It will keep for up to one month.

Per 1½ tablespoons: 14 calories; 0g protein; 0g fat; 0g saturated fat; 3g carbohydrates; 3.2g sugar; 0.6g fiber; 0.02g sodium

apple, plum, and date chutney

MAKES ABOUT 3¼ POUNDS

18 ounces ready-to-eat dried apple
  slices, roughly chopped (about 3 cups)

1 large onion, chopped

13 ounces plums, pitted and roughly
  chopped (about 2 cups)

¼ cup dates, chopped

2 teaspoons salt

1¼ cups white vinegar

⅔ cups minus 2 teaspoons Splenda
  granulated sweetener

6 cloves

1 cinnamon stick

This fruity chutney is perfect for serving with cold cuts and cheese.

Put the apples into a large pot and cover with 4 cups just-boiled water. Bring to a boil, then reduce the heat and simmer gently for about an hour until the water has almost evaporated.

Add the remaining ingredients and cook gently, stirring often, until the chutney is thick and pulpy–this will take about 45 minutes. Make sure the chutney is the thickness you want at this point, as it will only thicken a little more as it cools.

Remove the cinnamon stick, then can the chutney in warm, sterilized jars (see page 76) and seal while hot. Cool, then keep refrigerated and use within one month.

Per 1½ tablespoons: 22 calories; 0g protein; 0g fat; 0g saturated fat; 6g carbohydrates; 5.5g sugar; 0.8g fiber; 0.06g sodium

applesauce

SERVES 4

1 large cooking apple
2 eating apples
1 teaspoon Splenda granulated
   sweetener

Melinda says: This is one of those sauces that is easy to prepare, yet so versatile. It makes a great accompaniment to a variety of sweet and savory dishes.

Peel and core all apples and chop finely. Toss in the sweetener, then put into a small saucepan with the water.

Place the pan over a low heat and gently bring to a boil. Cover and simmer, keeping the heat very low, until the apple is just soft.

Stir well and pour into a warmed serving bowl.

Per serving: 42 calories; 0g protein; 0g fat; 0g saturated fat; 10g carbohydrates; 10.4g sugar; 1.8g fiber; 0g sodium

occasional treats and seasonal goodies

wholewheat crêpes with simmered winter fruits

SERVES 4

for the crêpes:
scant cup wholewheat flour
pinch of salt
1 egg, beaten
1¼ cups lowfat milk
1 teaspoon Splenda granulated
  sweetener
vegetable oil, for frying

for the fruit filling:
1 orange
1 cup orange juice
2½ tablespoons ready-to-eat dried
  apricots, chopped
2½ tablespoons raisins or golden raisins
pinch of apple pie spice
1 apple, cored and sliced
2 plums, pitted and sliced
2 teaspoons cornstarch
1 tablespoon Splenda granulated
  sweetener

Try these healthy crêpes, made with wholewheat flour or, if you prefer, make them with plain white flour.

Place the flour and salt into a large bowl with the egg, milk, and sweetener. Beat together with a wire whisk to make a smooth crêpe batter.

To make the filling, peel strips of zest from the orange using a potato peeler. Reserve 3 tablespoons of the orange juice, and pour the rest into a saucepan. Add the strips of zest, the apricots, raisins, and apple pie spice. Place on the heat and simmer gently for 10–15 minutes to plump up the fruit, then remove the orange zest. While the fruits simmer cut the orange into segments, removing all the pith, and set aside.

Drop the orange segments into the saucepan along with the sliced apple and plums. Mix the cornstarch with the reserved orange juice and add to the pan. Heat again gently, stirring until thickened and smooth. Stir in the sweetener, and keep it warm over a low heat while making the crêpes.

Heat a large frying pan and add a few drops of vegetable oil. Pour in a thin stream of batter, tilting the pan so that it flows evenly across the surface. Cook over a medium heat until set, then flip the crêpe over to cook the other side. Make four large crêpe in this way. Place on warm plates and serve immediately with the simmered fruit.

Per serving: 252 calories; 9g protein; 5g fat; 0.9g saturated fat; 45g carbohydrates; 25.2g sugar; 4.6g fiber; 0.21g sodium

hot cross buns

MAKES 10

2¾ cups white bread flour, plus extra
  for dusting
¾ cup mixed dried fruit
finely grated zest of 1 lemon
2 teaspoons apple pie spice
1 teaspoon ground cinnamon
1 x ¼-ounce envelope active dry yeast
6 tablespoons Splenda granulated
  sweetener
1 egg, beaten
3½ tablespoons unsalted butter, melted,
  plus extra for greasing
scant cup warm milk
oil, for greasing

for the crosses:
3 tablespoons flour
2–3 tablespoons milk
1 egg, beaten

Although easy to make, you'll need to allow plenty of time for the second rising of these spicy buns—they're made using a rich, fruity bread dough which takes longer to rise than a plainer dough. Once made, you can freeze any buns you won't be eating, warming them through in a moderate oven once thawed.

Put the bread flour, dried fruit, lemon zest, spices, yeast, and 4 tablespoons of the sweetener in a mixing bowl and stir to combine. Add the egg, melted butter, and milk, and mix with a round-bladed knife to make a soft dough.

Turn out onto a floured surface and knead for 10 minutes until the dough is smooth and elastic. Place in a lightly oiled bowl, cover with plastic wrap and let rise in a warm place for about 2 hours until the dough has doubled in size.

Lightly grease a large baking sheet. Punch down the dough and tip it onto a lightly floured counter. Divide into ten even-sized pieces and shape each into a ball. Place on the baking sheet, about 1¼ inches apart, and flatten them slightly. Cover with greased plastic wrap and let rise again for about 45 minutes until doubled in size.

Preheat the oven to 425°F.

To make the crosses, mix the plain flour with the milk to make a soft paste. Spoon into a small plastic bag and squeeze the mixture into a corner. Brush the dough with beaten egg. Snip off the corner of the bag and pipe crosses onto the buns. Bake in the oven for 15–20 minutes until risen and golden.

Dissolve the remaining sweetener in 2 teaspoons hot water. Transfer the buns to a wire rack and brush with the glaze. Let cool.

Per serving: 227 calories; 6g protein; 6g fat; 3.2g saturated fat; 40g carbohydrates; 9.3g sugar; 1.5g fiber; 0.17g sodium

easter egg brownies

MAKES 12

3½ ounces good-quality dark chocolate,
   chopped (about ⅔ cup)
½ cup (1 stick) unsalted butter
3 eggs
⅓ cup minus 1 teaspoon Splenda
   granulated sweetener
3 tablespoons flour
2 tablespoons cocoa powder
1 teaspoon baking powder
4½ ounces milk chocolate, chopped
   (about ¾ cup)

for the topping:
6 ounces milk chocolate (about 1 cup)
36 chocolate mini eggs

In this recipe, rich chocolate brownies are baked as individual cupcakes and finished with a chocolate mini egg topping. Like all chocolate brownie mixtures, they need very little cooking or they'll lose their moist texture.

Preheat the oven to 375°F. Line a muffin pan with 12 paper muffin cups.

Put the dark chocolate and butter in the top of a double boiler over barely simmering water. Stir frequently until the chocolate and butter are melted and mixed together. Alternatively, melt in the microwave and stir together.

Crack the eggs into a bowl and gradually beat in the sweetener until combined, then beat in the melted chocolate mixture. Sift the flour, cocoa powder, and baking powder into the bowl. Add the chopped milk chocolate and stir the ingredients together until just combined.

Divide the mixture into the paper cups and bake in the oven for about 8 minutes or until just firm. Transfer to a wire rack to cool.

To decorate the brownies, shave just over half of the milk chocolate into small curls using a potato peeler and set aside. If the chocolate breaks off in brittle shards, pop it in the microwave for a few seconds and try again.

Melt the remaining milk chocolate and spread it over the brownies. Top with the chocolate curls and the chocolate mini eggs. Delicious!

Per serving: 325 calories; 5g protein; 23g fat; 11.8g saturated fat; 27g carbohydrates; 23.4g sugar; 0.9g fiber; 0.11g sodium

star anise crème brûlée

SERVES 4

2½ cups cream
3 star anise
6 large egg yolks
2 tablespoons Splenda granulated
   sweetener
sugar, for sprinkling

This dessert is a classic with a hint of the Orient. It needs to be refrigerated overnight, so a bit of organization is required, but it's worth it for what is probably the greatest of British desserts.

Put the cream and star anise into a saucepan and place over the heat. You want the cream to become quite hot, but you don't want to bring it to a boil. Remove the pan from the heat and let stand for 30 minutes to allow the flavors to permeate.

Beat the egg yolks and sweetener together. Strain the flavored cream onto the egg mixture, whisk thoroughly, and return to the heat. Cook over a medium heat and stir constantly with a wooden spoon. Don't use a whisk as you don't want to incorporate air into the custard. Cook until the custard coats the back of a spoon. (A good test is to cover the back of a spoon with the custard, then run your finger down the middle of the spoon; if the custard does not join up again, it is ready.) Keep a close eye on the pan, making sure the custard doesn't come to a boil, otherwise it will split and separate, producing rather expensive scrambled eggs.

Strain the custard into four largish ramekins and let cool, then place in the fridge and leave overnight.

A couple of hours before serving, preheat the broiler and sprinkle each ramekin with a thin layer of sugar. Place the ramekins in an ice-filled tray and glaze the sugar under the broiler until caramelized with delicious dark patches. Once the sugar has been caramelized, don't refrigerate the dishes again.

To serve, crack open the caramel and indulge.

Per serving: 891 calories; 8g protein; 91g fat; 48g saturated fat; 11g carbohydrates; 11.1g sugar; 0g fiber; 0.05g sodium

balsamic strawberries with mascarpone cream

SERVES 12

1 pound, 10 ounces ripe strawberries,
hulled (about 7 cups)

¼ cup aged balsamic vinegar

2 tablespoons **Splenda** granulated
sweetener

for the mascarpone cream:

1 tablespoon **Splenda** granulated
sweetener

3 egg yolks

4 teaspoons kirsch

8 ounces mascarpone cheese
(about 1 cup)

⅓ cup heavy cream

**The strawberries you find in the stores these days often need a little
something to bring out their natural sweetness. In this recipe, the
Splenda and balsamic vinegar help to do just that.**

Mix the strawberries, balsamic vinegar, and sweetener together and let them
marinate for around 30 minutes.

To make the mascarpone cream, beat together the sweetener and the egg
yolks until the mixture has lightened to a pale yellow. Fold in the kirsch and
the mascarpone. Using clean beaters, beat the heavy cream until it forms soft
peaks, and fold gently into the mascarpone mixture.

To serve the strawberries, scoop them into bowls and top with a generous
spoonful of the mascarpone cream.

Per serving: 191 calories; 2g protein; 17g fat; 9.7g saturated fat; 6g carbohydrates;
6.4g sugar; 0.7g fiber; 0.03g sodium

orange and cardamom ice milk

SERVES 3

1 cup whole milk
finely grated zest of 2 oranges
1/3 cup plus 2 teaspoons Splenda
   granulated sweetener
1/2 vanilla sugar
1 tablespoon orange liqueur
1 egg
pinch of ground cardamom
2 1/2 cups buttermilk

Good oranges and the tang of buttermilk make this a sublime ice milk, which is as refreshing after a big winter dinner as it is in the heat of summer.

Take a large heavy saucepan and add all the ingredients except the buttermilk. Stir very thoroughly to make a lump-free custard and heat this over low heat, stirring frequently, until the mixture thickens to a light creamy consistency. This will take about 20 minuts or so.

Pour in the buttermilk and stir to blend the mixture thoroughly until it is fully incorporated. Cook for a few minutes more but do not boil. Remove from the heat and let cool, covered.

Once cool, chill for a couple of hours in the fridge, then scoop into a ice-cream maker, 1–1.5 quarts in size, and follow the manufacturer's instructions to churn and freeze.

Per serving: 326 calories; 12g protein; 6g fat; 3.2g saturated fat; 57g carbohydrates; 56.5g sugar; 0g fiber; 0.17g sodium

lemon syllabub with red fruits

SERVES 4

for the syllabub:
½ cup dry white wine
¼ cup brandy
finely grated zest and juice of 1 lemon
1 tablespoon honey
1¼ cups heavy cream
pinch of grated nutmeg

for the red fruits:
9 ounces strawberries, hulled and
    quartered (about 2-2½ cups)
8 ounces raspberries (about 1¾-2 cups)
5 ounces blackberries (about 1-1¼ cups)
1 cup red currants, stems removed and
    discarded
½ cup crème de cassis liqueur
2 tablespoons Splenda granulated
    sweetener
1 tablespoon lemon juice

Syllabubs have been eaten in England for hundreds of years and this tangy lemon one makes a wonderful complement to the sweetness of the red fruits. Great on a hot summer's evening after a barbeque.

Place the wine, brandy, 1 teaspoon lemon zest, the lemon juice, and honey in a nonreactive bowl and leave overnight for the flavors to mingle and develop.

The next day, add the cream and nutmeg and beat with a beater until the syllabub holds its shape. Pour into a glass bowl and refrigerate.

In another glass bowl, combine all the fruits gently with the liqueur, sweetener, and lemon juice. Leave them for about 3 hours, turning the fruits from time to time, before serving.

Serve the syllabub and fruits in their separate bowls and let your guests combine or eat separately as they wish. A very refreshing combination.

Per serving: 589 calories; 3g protein; 46g fat; 22.6g saturated fat; 22g carbohydrates; 21.7g sugar; 4.1g fiber; 0.05g sodium

lime, lemongrass, and mint jellos

SERVES 4

1 lemongrass stalk, cut into short
   lengths
a handful of fresh mint leaves
1½ tablespoons granulated gelatin
finely grated zest and juice of 2 limes
3 tablespoons Splenda granulated
   sweetener
¼ cup ginger, lemongrass, or
   elderflower syrup
lime slices, for decoration

These sophisticated jellos are meant for adults— though children might like them, too!

Bash the pieces of lemongrass with a rolling pin to bruise them, then put them into a saucepan with 6 of the mint leaves and 1 cup water. Simmer gently for 15 minutes, or until the liquid has reduced by about half.

Strain the hot lemongrass-flavored liquid through a strainer into a large measuring cup and stir in the granulated gelatin. Let it dissolve for 5–6 minutes, stirring occasionally to give a completely clear liquid.

Stir the lime zest, lime juice, and sweetener into the lemongrass liquid. Add the syrup, then pour in enough water to bring the level up to 3 cups. Pour into 4 glasses, then transfer to the fridge to chill and set. This will take about 3 hours.

Serve the jellos decorated with the remaining mint leaves and the lime slices.

Per serving: 56 calories; 4g protein; 0g fat; 0g saturated fat; 11g carbohydrates; 10.3g sugar; 0g fiber; 0.02g sodium

melon and ginger granita

SERVES 6

18 ounces melon (weighed
   without skin and seeds), cut into
   chunks (about 2½ cups)
2 tablespoons lemon juice
3 pieces preserved ginger in syrup,
   plus 3 tablespoons syrup from the jar
1¼ cups unsweetened apple juice
⅓ cup plus 2 teaspoons Splenda
   granulated sweetener

**Ice cool and so refreshing, this sophisticated granita is perfect for a
hot summer's day.**

Put the melon chunks into a blender with the lemon juice, 1 piece of preserved
ginger, the apple juice, and sweetener. Blend until very smooth. (You may have
to do this in batches.) Finely chop the remaining preserved ginger and stir into
the melon puree.

Tip the mixture into an icecream maker and follow the manufacturer's
instructions to freeze the mixture. Alternatively, tip into a freezer container and
freeze for about 1 hour. Stir with a fork to break up the ice crystals, then freeze
again for another hour. Repeat the stirring, then freeze until solid.

Remove the container from the freezer about 25 minutes before you wish to
serve the granita–you can tell it's ready when you can break it up with a fork.
Scoop into chilled glasses or bowls and serve immediately.

Per serving: 43 calories; 0g protein; 0g fat; 0g saturated fat; 11g carbohydrates;
10.7g sugar; 0.3g fiber; 0.02g sodium

tiramisù

SERVES 6

3 eggs, separated

2 tablespoons Splenda granulated
sweetener

9 ounces mascarpone cheese (about
1 cup)

1¼ cups Tia Maria liqueur

1¼ cups cold strong black coffee (real
coffee is best)

8 ounces ladyfingers

dark chocolate (minimum 70% cocoa
solids), grated, for decoration

Melinda says: Tiramisù is my ultimate dinner party dessert. It's a classic Italian dish and with this recipe, it takes almost no time to prepare, which leaves me with more time to spend with my guests!

Place the egg yolks and sweetener into a bowl. Beat thoroughly until the mixture lightens and thickens slightly, then stir in the mascarpone. Using clean beaters, beat the egg whites until stiff and fold them in, a little at a time.

Mix the liqueur with the coffee and dip half the ladyfingers into the liquid to soak them. Use the soaked fingers to line the bottom of a shallow dish, then spoon over them just over half of the mascarpone mixture. Dip the remaining ladyfingers in the liquid and make another layer, finishing off with the remaining mascarpone mixture.

Chill for a few hours (longer if you can–the flavours will mature the longer you leave it) and sprinkle with grated chocolate just before serving.

Per serving: 435 calories; 8g protein; 27g fat; 15.1g saturated fat; 37g carbohydrates; 24.1g sugar; 0.9g fiber; 0.11g sodium

black currant fool

1 pound fresh black currants (about 4¼-4½ cups)

2 tablespoons Splenda granulated sweetener

²/₃ cup heavy cream

²/₃ cup yogurt

4 sprigs fresh mint

A fool is a fruit puree and whipped cream dessert, and the intense flavor of fresh black currants makes a sublime fool. Black currants are also full of goodness—lots of vitamin C (perhaps three times as much as in oranges) and antioxidants called anthocyanins, which give black currants their deep, dark color.

Wash the black currants and remove the stalks. You can do this easily by running a fork down them.

Put the black currants and sweetener into a saucepan, add ¼ cup of water and bring gently to a boil. Simmer for around 15 minutes, stirring occasionally, until the fruit is well softened and the sweetener completely dissolved.

Push the black currants through a food mill or blitz them in a blender for a few seconds, then strain them through a fine mesh strainer to remove the seeds from the fruit. Set the puree aside to cool.

Beat the cream until it is good and thick, and then whisk in the yogurt, a spoonful at a time. Gently fold the creamy mixture into the fruit puree until barely blended—you don't want to knock all the air out of it, and a little marbling looks pretty, too.

Chill well in the fridge and serve in individual glasses, decorated with the sprigs of mint.

Per serving: 240 calories; 4g protein; 21g fat; 11.5g saturated fat; 11g carbohydrates; 11.1g sugar; 4g fiber; 0.04g sodium

tia maria mousse

SERVES 6

1 tablespoon granulated gelatin

7 tablespoons Splenda granulated
sweetener

1 teaspoon instant coffee powder or
freeze-dried granules

2 eggs, separated

¼ cup Tia Maria liqueur

²/₃ cup whipping cream

½ teaspoon cocoa powder

This light yet indulgent mousse is everything a yummy dessert should be.

Pour ²/₃ cup of very hot, but not boiling, water into a bowl and sprinkle the gelatin over it. Give it a stir, then let it dissolve for about 5 minutes until you have a completely clear liquid.

Meanwhile, put 5 tablespoons of the sweetener into a small saucepan with the instant coffee powder or granules and 4 teaspoons of water. Heat gently for a few seconds until the sweetener and coffee have dissolved.

Beat the egg whites in a grease-free bowl until stiff. Slowly add the coffee liquid, beating it in well.

Put the egg yolks, the rest of the sweetener and the liqueur into the top of a double boiler. Place over a saucepan gently simmering water and beat with a hand-held electric beater until thick and frothy. This will take at least 5 minutes. Fold in the egg white mixture and dissolved gelatin.

Whip the cream until thick, then fold about two thirds of it through the mixture. Divide the mousse between six glasses and chill in the fridge until set–this will take about 2 hours. Just before serving, top the desserts with the remaining whipped cream and sprinkle with the cocoa powder.

Per serving: 166 calories; 4g protein; 12g fat; 6.7g saturated fat; 5g carbohydrates; 4.8g sugar; 0g fiber; 0.04g sodium

christmas cake

2¼ pounds mixed dried fruit (about
   7-7½ cups)

⅔ cup candied cherries, cut in half

⅔ cup brandy or dark rum, plus 3
   tablespoons

¾ cup (1½ sticks) butter, softened,
   plus extra for greasing

½ cup plus 2 tablespoons Splenda
   granulated sweetener

4 eggs

2 tablespoons black treacle
   (or molasses)

finely grated zest and juice of 1 small
   orange

1 cup ground almonds

¾ cup flour

¼ teaspoon salt

1 teaspoon apple pie spice

for the frosting:

¼ cup apricot baking glaze or
   strained apricot jam

confectioners' sugar, for dusting

18 ounces marzipan (about 1⅔ cups)

1 pound, 10 ounces ready-rolled
   fondant icing

Make this cake a couple of days before Christmas and use within ten days—it will not keep as long as a traditional cake.

The day before baking the cake, put the dried fruit, cherries, and rum or brandy into a large bowl. Stir well and cover. Soak for 24 hours, stirring occasionally.

The next day, grease an 8-inch round cake pan with high sides and line with a double layer of parchment paper. Preheat the oven to 300°F. In a very large bowl, beat the butter and sweetener together until light and creamy. Beat in the eggs, one by one, then stir in the treacle. Add the orange zest, juice, and ground almonds. Sift in the flour, salt, and apple pie spice, then fold in using a large metal spoon. Stir in the soaked dried fruit, mixing thoroughly.

Tip the fruited batter into the prepared pan and level with the back of a spoon. Bake for about 2¼ hours. After 2 hours, cover with a double layer of parchment paper or foil to prevent it from getting too dark. To check whether the cake is done, insert a skewer into the middle of the cake—it should come out clean. If not, bake for a little longer.

Put the cake pan on a wire rack to cool completely, then remove the cake from the pan. Spoon over the extra 3 tablespoons brandy or rum over the cake, letting it soak in. Warm the apricot glaze or jam, then brush it all over the cake. Dust your counter with confectioners' sugar and roll out half the marzipan into a long strip. Trim it to fit around the sides of the cake and place in position. Roll out the remaining marzipan into a circle and fit it on top of the cake. Cover with plastic wrap and let harden for 24 hours.

The following day, dust your counter and a rolling pin with confectioners' sugar. Roll out the ready-rolled icing and continue to roll until it's large enough to cover the top and sides of the cake. Blanket the cake with the rolled icing, smoothing it with your hands. Trim off any excess and decorate to your liking.

Per serving: 587 calories; 6g protein; 16g fat; 5.4g saturated fat; 105g carbohydrates; 93g sugar; 2.8g fiber; 0.15g sodium

everyday desserts

apple pie

SERVES 6

3½ tablespoons unsalted butter, plus
   extra for greasing

1 large cooking apple, peeled, cored,
   and sliced

4 dessert apples, peeled, cored, and
   sliced

3 tablespoons Splenda granulated
   sweetener

10 cloves

1½ teaspoons apple pie spice

2 tablespoons fresh lemon juice

13 ounces sweet pie dough or puff
   pastry dough

flour, for dusting

1 egg, beaten

This is a double crust apple pie that's best made on a metal pie plate so the bottom has a chance to crisp up.

Preheat the oven to 400°F, adding a baking sheet to heat through. Grease an 8½-inch pie plate.

Melt half the butter in a large frying pan. Add the apples and sweetener and cook gently for 5 minutes, stirring frequently, until the apples start to soften. Stir in the spices and lemon juice and let cool.

Roll out half the dough on a lightly floured surface and line the pie plate with it. Scatter the apples and juices over the top, piling them up in the center. Dot with the remaining butter. Brush the rim of the dough with the beaten egg.

Roll out the remaining dough and cover the pie with it. Press the edges together along the rim using the tines of a fork to seal. Trim off any excess dough and use to decorate the top if you like. Make a few slashes in the top with a sharp knife–this will allow the steam to escape. Brush the top with more beaten egg and bake in the oven for 35–40 minutes until pale golden.

Per serving: 348 calories; 4g protein; 22g fat; 10.3g saturated fat; 36g carbohydrates; 13g sugar; 1.8g fiber; 0.2g sodium

rhubarb free-form pie

SERVES 6

3½ tablespoons cold butter, cut into
    cubes, plus extra for greasing

1²/₃ cups flour, plus extra for dusting
pinch of salt

5 tablespoons vegetable shortening
    (for dough-making), cut into cubes

1 egg, beaten

2½ tablespoons ground semolina

1½ pounds rhubarb, trimmed
    and chopped

½ cup Splenda granulated
    sweetener

In this pie the rhubarb is simply encased in a loosely formed crust—meaning you don't have to be too precise with your rolling and measuring.

Preheat the oven to 375°F. Lightly grease a large baking tray with a little butter.

Sift the flour and salt into a bowl. Add the butter and vegetable fat and rub together with your fingertips until the mixture resembles fine breadcrumbs. Add just enough cold water to make a smooth, but not sticky, dough. Wrap in clingfilm and refrigerate for 10–15 minutes.

Roll out the dough on a lightly floured counter to form a circle measuring about 14 inches across. Lift carefully onto the baking tray. Brush the surface with beaten egg and sprinkle the semolina over the middle, to within 3 inches of the edge. This will help to soak up the juices from the fruit, helping to prevent a soggy crust.

Mix the rhubarb and sweetener together, then pile on top of the semolina. Draw up the edges of the dough around the fruit, overlapping where necessary and pressing together. Don't expect the dough to cover the fruit.

Brush the dough again with beaten egg. Bake on the middle shelf for 25–30 minutes, until golden brown. Serve warm with custard, ice cream, or plain yogurt.

Per serving: 307 calories; 6g protein; 17g fat; 6.8g saturated fat; 35g carbohydrates; 3.5g sugar; 2.9g fiber; 0.17g sodium

bananas in citrus rum sauce

SERVES 4

3 tablespoons butter

6 bananas (not too ripe), thickly sliced

finely grated zest and juice of 1 large
  orange

2 tablespoons Splenda granulated
  sweetener

1/3 cup raisins or golden raisins

3 tablespoons rum or brandy

1–2 tablespoons slivered almonds,
  toasted

For a quick, delicious dessert, this recipe comes up trumps!

Melt the butter in a large frying pan and add the bananas. Cook them for a minute or so over medium heat to warm them through. Make sure you don't overcook them, or else they will go soggy.

Add 1 teaspoon orange zest, the orange juice, sweetener, and raisins to the pan. Cook over a low heat, stirring gently, for 1 minute. Remove the pan from the heat and stir in the rum or brandy, then place back on the heat to let the sauce bubble for a moment or two. Scatter the almonds on top, then serve at once.

Per serving: 296 calories; 3g protein; 10g fat; 5.5g saturated fat; 46g carbohydrates; 42.4g sugar; 2.1g fiber; 0.07g sodium

greek lemon custards

SERVES 4

11 ounces cream cheese (about ¹/₃ cup)

finely grated zest of 1 large lemon

¼ cup Splenda granulated sweetener

9 ounces 0% fat Greek yogurt
  (about 1-1¼ cups)

1 teaspoon vanilla extract

2 large eggs, beaten

6 ounces fresh or thawed frozen
  raspberries (about 1½ cups)

Make these delightful custards in individual custard cups or ramekins—it makes serving them much easier.

Preheat the oven to 350°F.

Beat the cream cheese and lemon zest together until combined, then beat in the sweetener, yogurt, and vanilla extract. Strain the beaten eggs through a fine mesh strainer into the cheese mixture and beat well.

Pour the mixture into four individual custard cups or ramekins. Place the custard cups in a large, deep roasting pan and pour in enough warm water to come halfway up their side to make a water bath. Transfer carefully to the oven and bake for 25–30 minutes, until set.

Serve the custards warm or chilled, topped with the raspberries.

Per serving: 182 calories; 19g protein; 8g fat; 3.4g saturated fat; 10g carbohydrates; 8.2g sugar; 1.4g fiber; 0.39g sodium

kiwi and grape cheesecake layer

SERVES 4

9 sheets (18 squares) graham crackers, crushed

¼ cup marsala or sweet sherry

2 kiwis, peeled and sliced

9 ounces seedless grapes, cut in half (about 1²/₃ cups)

7 ounces cream cheese (a scant cup)

11 ounces Greek-style plain yogurt (about 1¹/₃-1½ cups)

2 tablespoons Splenda granulated sweetener

½ teaspoon vanilla extract

You won't believe how delicious this simple, layered dessert tastes—so why not make it to find out?

Take half the graham cracker crumbs over and divide them into individual glasses. Sprinkle 1 tablespoon of marsala or sherry evenly into each one.

Mix the kiwi slices with the grapes and spoon half the fruit into the glasses.

Beat the cream cheese with a wooden spoon until creamy and soft, then mix in the yogurt, sweetener, and vanilla extract. Spoon this mixture into the glasses, on top of the fruit.

Sprinkle the remaining graham cracker crumbs on top, followed by the rest of the fruit. Cover and chill until ready to serve.

Per serving: 359 calories; 13g protein; 16g fat; 8.3g saturated fat; 40g carbohydrates; 22.3g sugar; 1.4g fiber; 0.44g sodium

frozen berry yogurt

SERVES 8

1 pound frozen mixed berries or
raspberries (about 3½-4 cups)

²/₃ cup minus 2 teaspoons Splenda
granulated sweetener

18 ounces Greek-style plain yogurt
(about 2¹/₃ cups)

2 teaspoons vanilla extract

Frozen mixed fruits are available in most supermarkets and great for this easy dessert.

Put the frozen berries into a blender or food processor. Add the sweetener, yogurt, and vanilla extract, and blend for about 20 seconds until combined.

Tip the mixture into an icecream maker and follow the manufacturer's instructions to freeze. Alternatively, tip the mixture into a rigid freezer container and freeze for about 1 hour. Remove and stir with a fork to break up the ice crystals, then refreeze. In another hour, stir it again, and then again one hour after that, then freeze the mixture until solid.

Remove the container from the freezer about 30 minutes before serving so the mixture can soften a little. Scoop into chilled glasses and serve.

Per serving: 100 calories; 5g protein; 6g fat; 3.6g saturated fat; 8g carbohydrates; 7.7g sugar; 1.5g fiber; 0.05g sodium

coffee panna cotta

SERVES 6

6 sheets leaf gelatin (⅓ ounce in total)
⅓ cup plus 2 teaspoons Baileys
   Irish Cream
7 ounces cream cheese (scant cup)
1 teaspoon vanilla extract
1¼ cups milk
scant ½ cup light cream
⅔ cup strong black coffee
2 tablespoons Splenda granulated
   sweetener

The Irish Cream liqueur gives this lovely dessert some added oomph!

Use a pair of scissors to snip the sheets of leaf gelatin into a shallow bowl. Spoon the liqueur over them and leave for 5 minutes, until slightly softened.

Meanwhile, put the cream cheese, vanilla extract and 2 tablespoons of the milk into a saucepan and whisk until smooth. Stir in the remaining milk and the cream to give a smooth liquid. Heat gently, stirring all the time, until hot but not boiling. Remove from the heat and add the gelatin and liqueur. Stir until the gelatinhas dissolved, then mix in the coffee and sweetener.

Wet the insides of six 5-ounce custard cups or ramekins. Fill with the panna cotta mixture. Chill for about 3–4 hours, or overnight, until set.

To serve, dip the custard cups briefly into hot water and turn out onto pretty plates.

Per serving: 218 calories; 7g protein; 17g fat; 9g saturated fat; 7g carbohydrates; 7.1g sugar; 0g fiber; 0.16g sodium

rhubarb and ginger fool

SERVES 4

1¼ pounds rhubarb, trimmed and cut
  into 1-inch pieces (about 5-6 cups)
½ cup Splenda granulated
  sweetener
2 pieces preserved ginger in syrup,
  plus 2 tablespoons syrup from the jar
5 ounces mascarpone cheese (about ²/₃
  scant cup)
¼ cup Greek-style plain yogurt
4 gingersnaps, roughly crushed

Simple flavors combine to make an easy, sensational ersatz fool.

Put the rhubarb and sweetener into a large, shallow pan. Add ¼ cup of water and the preserved ginger syrup. Place on the heat and simmer gently, uncovered, for 6–8 minutes, until the rhubarb is tender but not mushy. Let cool.

Meanwhile, chop 1 piece of preserved ginger and finely slice the other.

Take half the rhubarb, with some of the juice from the pan, and divide it between four serving glasses.

Mix the remaining rhubarb, without its juice, with the mascarpone cheese and yogurt. Fold in the chopped preserved ginger and most of the crushed gingersnaps. Spoon the mixture into the serving glasses.

To decorate the desserts, sprinkle the reserved crushed gingersnaps and slices of preserved ginger over the top, then chill until ready to serve.

Per serving: 292 calories; 4g protein; 20g fat; 12.2g saturated fat; 25g carbohydrates; 19.8g sugar; 2.3g fiber; 0.09g sodium

strawberry soufflé omelet

SERVES 2

8 ounces strawberries (about 2 cups),
  hulled and cut in half
1 tablespoon fresh lemon juice
3 tablespoons Splenda granulated
  sweetener
4 eggs, separated
1 teaspoon vanilla extract
2 teaspoons butter

Soufflé omelets may sound quite special, yet they are a quick and easy way to produce a nutritious dessert.

Put the strawberries into a small saucepan. Add the lemon juice, half the sweetener, and 2 tablespoons of water. Heat gently until the fruit has softened slightly–this will take about 2 minutes. Turn the heat to very low.

Preheat the broiler to hot. In a large, grease-free bowl, beat the egg whites until they hold their shape. In a separate bowl, beat the egg yolks with the remaining sweetener and the vanilla extract. Fold the egg yolk mixture into the egg whites using a large metal spoon.

To make the first omelet, melt half the butter in a medium-sized nonstick omelet pan or frying pan. Add half the egg mixture and cook for about a minute until the bottom of the soufflé has set. Place the pan under the broiler for a few moments until the top has set and browned a little.

Slide onto a warm plate, fill with half the strawberries and fold the omelet over them. Keep it warm while you make the second omelet, then serve at once.

Per serving: 232 calories; 13g protein; 15g fat; 5.6g saturated fat; 10g carbohydrates; 10.4g sugar; 1.2g fiber; 0.18g sodium

french toast with fresh berry sauce

SERVES 2

for the french toast:

1 egg

²/₃ cup milk

1 teaspoon vanilla extract

1 tablespoon Splenda granulated sweetener

2 thick slices white bread, crusts removed

1¾ tablespoons butter

for the fresh berry sauce:

2½ ounces blueberries (about ½-²/₃ cup)

2½ ounces raspberries (about ½-²/₃ cup)

2½ strawberries, hulled and sliced (about ½ cup)

1 tablespoon Splenda granulated sweetener

Try this recipe for a fast, easy dessert or enjoy it as a satisfying, nutritious start to the day.

In a large shallow bowl, beat together the egg, milk, vanilla extract, and sweetener. Cut each slice of bread in half diagonally and add the pieces of bread to the egg mixture. Let them soak for about 5 minutes, turning them once.

Melt the butter in a large frying pan. Add the soaked bread and fry gently for 1–2 minutes until set and golden brown. Turn over the pieces and cook them on the other side for another 1–2 minutes.

Meanwhile, put the berries and remaining sweetener into a saucepan with 2 tablespoons water. Heat and simmer gently for 2–3 minutes. Serve with the hot French toast.

Per serving: 302 calories; 10g protein; 15g fat; 8.2g saturated fat; 33g carbohydrates; 14g sugar; 2.6g fiber; 0.35g sodium

fruity clafoutis

SERVES 4

1 teaspoon butter

1 apple, peeled, cored, and chopped

1 tablespoon fresh lemon juice

4 ready-to-eat dried apricots, roughly
chopped

3 plums, pitted and quartered

¼ cup golden raisins

2 eggs

1 cup milk

3 tablespoons Splenda granulated
sweetener

1 tablespoon flour

2–3 drops vanilla extract

**Clafoutis, a traditional French dessert made with a light batter, is
delicious with this selection of orchard fruits.**

Preheat the oven to 350°F. Grease a 5-cup shallow baking dish with the butter.

Mix together the apple, lemon juice, apricots, plums, and raisins. Tip them into
the baking dish and spread out in an even layer.

Using a wire whisk, beat together the eggs, milk, sweetener, flour, and vanilla
extract to make a smooth batter. Pour this over the fruit layer and place in the
oven.

Bake for 35–40 minutes until set and golden. Serve hot with light cream or plain
yogurt.

Per serving: 159 calories; 6g protein; 5g fat; 2g saturated fat; 24g carbohydrates;
20.8g sugar; 1.9g fiber; 0.07g sodium

hot mango and pineapple meringue pudding

SERVES 4

8-ounce can pineapple pieces in
   natural juice
3 tablespoons cornstarch
2 large eggs, separated
2 cups lowfat milk
1 teaspoon vanilla extract
¼ cup Splenda granulated sweetener
1 small mango, peeled, pitted and
   chopped

This easy pudding looks fabulous and tastes divine—you must try it!

Preheat the oven to 375°C.

Drain the pineapple juice into a medium-sized nonstick saucepan. Blend in the cornstarch, then stir in the egg yolks, milk, and vanilla extract. Heat, stirring all the time with a small whisk or wooden spoon, until the mixture boils and thickens.

Remove the pan from the heat and stir in half the sweetener. Add the pineapple pieces and chopped mango and stir well.

Spoon the mixture into a 5-cup baking dish or four individual ovenproof dishes. Place on a baking tray and bake for 5 minutes while you prepare the meringue topping.

Beat the egg whites in a grease-free bowl until they hold their shape. Add the remaining sweetener and beat again until the meringue is stiff. Pile onto the hot pudding and bake for a another 4–5 minutes until billowy and golden brown.

Per serving: 205 calories; 8g protein; 5g fat; 2g saturated fat; 33g carbohydrates; 22.1g sugar; 1.8g fiber; 0.1g sodium

mango and yogurt fool

SERVES 4

1 pound, 5 ounces Greek-style yogurt
   (about 2¾-3 cups)
1 tablespoon grated fresh peeled ginger
   (and the juices)
1 teaspoon ground cardamom
2 mangoes, peeled and pitted
²/₃ cup heavy cream
1 tablespoon Splenda granulated
   sweetener
½ teaspoon vanilla extract
strips of orange zest, for decorating

The combination of yogurt and mango works surprisingly well in this rich and tasty fool. The fruit in this fool is soft, so it doesn't need cooking before it goes into the dish.

Combine the yogurt with the ginger and its juices (grating the ginger over a bowl to catch them). Add in the ground cardamom.

Finely chop one of the mangoes and set it aside. Cut the flesh off the other one and puree it in a blender. For an extra smooth puree, pass it through a strainer or foodmill. Mix the chopped mango and the puree into the yogurt.

Whip the cream with the sweetener and vanilla extract until it forms soft peaks. Fold the cream into the mango yogurt and spoon the mixture into glasses. Refrigerate until needed.

Blanch the strips of orange zest quickly in boiling water for 1–2 minutes and let cool. Use these to decorate the fool. Serve in pretty individual glasses, well chilled.

Per serving: 442 calories; 11g protein; 34g fat; 19.9g saturated fat; 24g carbohydrates; 22.4g sugar; 3.4g fiber; 0.12g sodium

plum, fig, and blueberry fruit salad

SERVES 4

1 small unwaxed lemon

1 cinnamon stick

¼ cup Splenda granulated sweetener

10 ounces plums, cut in half and pitted

1½ cups blueberries

4 fresh figs, quartered

Fruit salads are delicious and so good for you—and this one combines some great flavors.

Cut a wide strip of lemon zest from the lemon using a speed peeler and put into a saucepan. Squeeze the lemon and add the juice to the pan along with the cinnamon stick, sweetener, and 1 cup of water. Place on the burner and simmer gently for 2 minutes.

Add the plums to the saucepan and simmer gently for another 5–6 minutes, until tender. Remove the saucepan from the heat and add the blueberries. Let cool for 10 minutes, then discard the strip of lemon zest and the cinnamon stick.

Add the figs to the plum mixture, stir everything together gently, then serve barely warm or chilled.

Per serving: 72 calories; 1g protein; 0g fat; 0g saturated fat; 17g carbohydrates; 16.8g sugar; 2.9g fiber; 0g sodium

raspberry cranachan

SERVES 4

½ cup rolled oats (old-fashioned oats)
8 ounces raspberries (about 1¾-2 cups)
1¼ cups heavy cream
2 tablespoons Splenda granulated
    sweetener

Cranachan is a luxury version of the Scottish crowdie, developed for eating at harvest festivals and using cream instead of water or buttermilk. For a lighter version, replace the whipped cream with Greek-style yogurt. For this recipe we're using rolled oats instead of the traditional steel-cut oats.

Preheat the broiler. Sprinkle the rolled oats onto a baking tray and spread them out evenly. Carefully toast them until they are light brown–this will take 2–3 minutes. Keep a close eye on them to make sure that they don't burn. Cool completely.

Put half the raspberries into a bowl. Use a fork or potato masher to crush them lightly. Put the remaining whole raspberries into four serving glasses, reserving some for decoration.

In a large chilled mixing bowl, whip the cream until thick. Tip in the crushed raspberries and toasted oats. Add the sweetener and stir together gently. There's no need to mix everything thoroughly–a random, marbled effect will look great.

Spoon the cream mixture into the serving glasses and decorate with the reserved raspberries. Cover and chill until ready to serve.

Per serving: 436 calories; 4g protein; 41g fat; 22.8g saturated fat; 13g carbohydrates; 4.6g sugar; 2.7g fiber; 0.02g sodium

rice pudding

SERVES 4

¼ cup short-grain rice

⅓ cup nonfat dry milk

2 tablespoons Splenda granulated
   sweetener

2½ cups lowfat milk

1 teaspoon ground nutmeg

strawberry jam, for serving

Melinda says: This recipe is a great everyday dish. You can keep it simple, or follow my tip for extra flavor by adding a spoonful of strawberry conserve on top.

Preheat the oven to 300°F.

Place the rice, dry milk, sweetener, and milk in a 1-quart ovenproof dish. Mix together and then smooth out evenly.

Sprinkle half the ground nutmeg over it and place on the middle shelf of the oven.

Bake for 45 minutes, then remove the dish from the oven and either stir in the skin that has formed on top, or remove it.

Sprinkle the remaining nutmeg over it and return it to the oven.

Bake for another 45 minutes until the top is golden brown, the rice is soft, and most of the liquid has been absorbed. Serve hot or cold with a few teaspoons of strawberry jam.

Per serving: 588 calories; 55g protein; 1g fat; 0.6g saturated fat; 95g carbohydrates; 85.4g sugar; 0g fiber; 0.83g sodium

apricot fool

SERVES 4

18 ounces fresh apricots, cut in half
and pitted

1 tablespoon Splenda granulated
sweetener

1½ cups heavy cream

mint leaves, for decoration (optional)

The flavor of a warm, ripe apricot picked off a tree in the sunshine stays with you for life! Combined into a fool, this makes a very pleasing pudding.

Place the apricot halves into a saucepan with the sweetener and ¼ cup of water. Bring to simmering point over a gentle heat, and continue cooking for about 5 minutes until the apricots are just softening.

The sweetness of this dish depends upon how ripe the fruit is and how sweet you like it, so taste and add some more sweetener if you think it needs it.

Put the apricots through a strainer or foodmill or blitz them for 30 seconds in a blender. Set aside to cool thoroughly.

Beat the cream until it forms soft peaks. Fold in the apricot puree. Serve well chilled and decorate with a few mint leaves if you like.

Per serving: 475 calories; 3g protein; 47g fat; 26.4g saturated fat; 11g carbohydrates; 10.8g sugar; 2.1g fiber; 0.02g sodium

scotch pancakes with blueberries

MAKES 10

generous ¾ cup flour

1 teaspoon baking powder

1 tablespoon Splenda granulated
   sweetener

1 egg

²/₃ cup lowfat milk

1½ tablespoons lightly salted
   butter, melted

1¼ cups fresh or frozen blueberries

1 tablespoon maple syrup

1 tablespoon sunflower oil

These pancakes are perfect for a leisurely breakfast or late morning snack. Serve as they are or topped with spoonfuls of crème fraîche or Greek yogurt.

Mix together the flour, baking powder, and sweetener in a bowl. Make a well in the center and break in the egg. Add a little of the milk and whisk with the egg, gradually incorporating the flour to make a smooth batter. Add the remaining milk and the butter and mix until smooth.

Put the blueberries and maple syrup in a small saucepan and heat gently until the blueberry juices start to run. Transfer to a small serving bowl.

Heat a small amount of the oil in a large, heavy frying pan. Pour a little of the batter into the pan so it spreads to a pancake about 3 inches in diameter. Pour in several more pancakes, leaving a little space between each and cook gently for 1 minute or until golden on the underside. Turn the pancakes with a spatula and cook for another minute. Remove to a warmed plate and repeat with the remaining batter, adding more oil to the pan when needed.

Pile the pancakes onto serving plates and sprinkle with a little more sweetener if you like. Serve with the blueberries.

Per serving: 87 calories; 2g protein; 4g fat; 1.5g saturated fat; 12g carbohydrates; 3.1g sugar; 0.6g fiber; 0.09g sodium

warm berries with sabayon sauce

SERVES 4

1¾ cups blueberries

3 tablespoons Splenda granulated sweetener

2 cups strawberries, hulled and cut in half

2 cups raspberries

2 egg yolks

¼ cup white grape juice or apple juice

¼ cup white wine

This simple summer dessert tastes sensational with its frothy white wine sauce.

Put the blueberries, 1 tablespoon sweetener, and 3 tablespoons cold water into a saucepan. Heat gently for 2–3 minutes until the juice begins to run from the fruit. Cool slightly, then mix gently with the strawberries and raspberries.

Using a hand-held electric beater, beat the egg yolks with the remaining sweetener in the top of a double boiler over gently simmering water until very pale in color and light in texture. Add the grape or apple juice, and white wine, and continue to beat until the sauce thickens. Remove from the heat and beat for another further 30 seconds or so.

Divide the fruit between individual serving dishes and spoon the sauce on top.

Per serving: 99 calories; 3g protein; 4g fat; 0.9g saturated fat; 13g carbohydrates; 12.9g sugar; 3g fiber; 0.01g sodium

family favorites

deep-filled pear pie with crème anglaise

SERVES 6

1⅔ cups flour, plus extra for dusting
pinch of salt
3½ tablespoons shortening,
3½ tablespoons cold butter, cut up
1 egg, beaten
juice of 1 lemon
1 pound, 10 ounces not too ripe pears
5 tablespoons Splenda granulated
  sweetener

for the crème anglaise:
1¼ cups whole milk
1¼ light cream
1 vanilla bean, split open lengthwise
4 large organic egg yolks
2 tablespoons Splenda granulated
  sweetener

Put the flour and salt into a bowl. Add the shortening and butter and rub in with your fingertips until the mixture looks like fine breadcrumbs. Add just enough cold water to make a soft, but not sticky dough. Knead lightly for a few moments until smooth, then wrap in plastic wrap or waxed paper and chill for 10 minutes.

Preheat the oven to 400°F. Divide the dough into two equal pieces. Roll out each piece on a lightly floured counter into a circle 10 inches across. Use one circle to line a 9-inch pie plate. Brush the bottom with a little beaten egg.

Squeeze the lemon juice into a bowl. Peel, core and slice the pears, and place into the bowl with the sweetener. Toss together and tip into the pie dish. Brush the edges of the pastry with a little water, then cover with the second pastry circle, pressing the edges together to seal. Trim with a sharp knife, then brush the surface with beaten egg.

Bake in the oven for 25–30 minutes, until the crust is golden brown. Meanwhile, make the crème anglaise. Place the milk, cream, and vanilla bean in a heavy saucepan and slowly bring to a boil. Remove from the heat and let infuse for 15 minutes.

Whisk the egg yolks with the sweetener in a bowl. Pour the cream mixture over the yolks, whisking well. Lift out the vanilla bean and, with a teaspoon, scrape the seeds back into the custard. Wash the saucepan and return the custard to the pan. Cook very gently over the lowest heat, stirring constantly until the sauce is thick enough to coat the back of the spoon. This will take about 8–10 minutes. Pour into a sauceboat.

Remove the pie from the oven and let cool for a few minutes. Serve with the crème anglaise.

Per serving: 499 calories; 11g protein; 33g fat; 14.9g saturated fat; 44g carbohydrates; 14.9g sugar; 2.5g fiber; 0.24g sodium

panettone and clementine bread and butter pudding

SERVES 6

3 tablespoons butter

6 slices (about 12 ounces) panettone or light raisin bread

3 clementines, peeled and thinly sliced

3 eggs

2½ cups lowfat milk

⅔ cup light cream

3 tablespoons Splenda granulated sweetener

1 teaspoon vanilla extract

pinch of ground nutmeg

Try this classic favorite with a twist—made with Italian panettone or raisin bread and sliced clementines. It's truly delicious.

Use a little of the butter to grease a 1.5 quart baking dish. Spread the rest of the butter over the slices of panettone or raisin bread. Cut the bread into triangles, then lay them in the dish, overlapping them to fit. Distribute the clementine slices among the bread slices.

Beat together the eggs, milk, cream, sweetener, and vanilla extract. Pour into the dish, over the bread. Cover with plastic wrap and leave it for at least 30 minutes. If you want to cook the pudding later, refrigerate until needed.

Preheat the oven to 350°F.

Sprinkle the bread pudding with the ground nutmeg. Bake in the oven for 30–35 minutes until puffed up and golden brown. Cool for a few minutes, then serve.

Per serving: 422 calories; 11g protein; 24g fat; 11.9g saturated fat; 42g carbohydrates; 28.8g sugar; 1.1g fiber; 0.24g sodium

apple and blackberry charlotte

SERVES 4

1 pound, 10 ounces baking apples,
  peeled, cored, and chopped (about
  5 cups)
finely grated zest and juice of 1 orange
pinch of ground cinnamon
7 ounces blackberries (about 1½ cups)
4-5 tablespoons Splenda granulated
  sweetener
3½ tablespoons butter, melted
7 slices white bread, crusts removed

Remind yourself just how good this traditional favorite tastes!

Preheat the oven to 350°F.

Put the apples into a saucepan with the orange zest, orange juice, and cinnamon. Add 5 tablespoons of water, then simmer uncovered until the apples are tender–this will take about 10 minutes. Stir in the blackberries, then sweeten to taste with the sweetener.

Brush a 6-inch round, high-sided baking dish with melted butter. Brush the rest of the butter over the bread slices. Place one slice in the bottom of the baking dish, reserve one for the top, then fit the rest of the slices around the sides, easing them into place and cutting them to fit so that there are no gaps.

Spoon the apple and blackberry mixture into the breadlined baking dish and place the remaining slice of bread on top, folding the bread around and over the sides to enclose the filling. Bake for 30–35 minutes. Cool for a few minutes, then serve.

Per serving: 299 calories; 5g protein; 12g fat; 6.7g saturated fat; 46g carbohydrates; 23.3g sugar; 5.3g fiber; 0.33g sodium

apple fritters

SERVES 4

for the batter:
generous ¾ cups all-purpose flour
1½ tablespoons butter, melted
1 egg yolk, plus 2 egg whites
½ tablespoon Splenda granulated
  sweetener
grated zest of 1 lemon
3 tablespoons dark rum, plus extra for
  serving
½ teaspoon salt

vegetable oil, for frying
1 pound eating apples, cored and peeled
confectioners' sugar, for dusting
  (optional)

This is something I used to have when I was a child. It brings back memories of all of us sitting around the table as a family. In our household, desserts were served daily—but those were the days when kids got much more exercise than today, just by playing outside.

Start by making the batter: beat together the flour, butter, 1 egg yolk, sweetener, lemon zest, rum, salt, and 3 tablespoons of water. Let the mixture stand in the fridge for 30 minutes.

Just before you're ready to fry your fritters, clean the beaters and then beat the egg whites in a grease-free bowl until they hold their shape, and fold them into the batter.

Fill a deep pan or deepfryer with vegetable oil and heat until hot.

Cut each apple into six wedges. Dip the wedges into the batter and fry a few at a time in the hot oil until nicely browned. Repeat until all are fried. Drain well on paper towels.

Sprinkle the fritters with a few drops of rum and dust them with confectioners' sugar if you like.

Per serving: 358 calories; 6g protein; 20g fat; 4.9g saturated fat; 34g carbohydrates; 13.4g sugar; 3.1g fiber; 0.32g sodium

pumpkin pie

SERVES 6

1 x 9-inch pie shell unbaked
18 ounces peeled and seeded
  pumpkin, cut into 1-inch chunks
  (about 4-4½ cups)
3 eggs
2 tablespoons brown sugar
2 tablespoons Splenda granulated
  sweetener
1½ teaspoons ground cinnamon
1 teaspoon ground ginger
½ teaspoon allspice
½ teaspoon ground cloves
¼ teaspoon ground cardamom
pinch of sea salt or kosher salt
thick plain yogurt, for the topping

Melinda says: This is one of my all time favorite pies. The mix of spices and flavors is just so comforting during the colder months.

Preheat the oven to 375°F. Prick the pie shell with a fork and line with a large piece of foil. Fill the foil with a single layer of baking beans or dried beans, then bake for 10–15 minutes. Lift out the foil and beans.

Turn the oven temperature up to 425°F.

To make the filling, steam the pumpkin until softened, then place in a strainer and press lightly to extract any excess water. Mash it into a puree.

In a large bowl, beat the eggs, sugar, and sweetener together until light and frothy. Add the mashed pumpkin, all the spices and the salt, and blend until thoroughly combined.

Pour into the pie shell and level the top of the filling roughly. Bake in the oven for around 8–10 minutes, then reduce the oven temperature to 325°F and continue baking for another 30 minutes or until the filling is set. To check that the pie is cooked, insert a skewer into the center and, if it comes out clean, the filling is cooked. Remove from the oven and let cool.

Spread the cake with the yogurt and sprinkle with a little extra cinnamon if you like. Keep in the fridge.

Per serving: 244 calories; 6g protein; 13g fat; 3.9g saturated fat; 27g carbohydrates; 10.6g sugar; 1.4g fiber; 0.25g sodium

lemon meringue pie

SERVES 6

1 x 8-inch sweet pie shell ready-baked

3 tablespoons cornstarch

finely grated zest and juice of 2 large
  lemons

5 tablespoons Splenda granulated
  sweetener

2 large eggs, separated

Make a quick version of this popular dessert by using a store-bought pie shell—though of course you could make your own, if you prefer.

Preheat the oven to 350°F. Place the pie shell onto a baking tray and set aside.

In a small nonstick saucepan, blend the cornstarch with a scant cup cold water. Add the lemon zest and juice and bring to a boil, stirring constantly until the mixture thickens. Remove from the heat and stir in 4 tablespoons of the sweetener. Cool for about 10 minutes, stirring often to prevent a skin from forming.

Mix the egg yolks into the lemon mixture, then pour into the pie shell. Bake in the oven for 12–15 minutes, until set.

Beat the egg whites in a grease-free bowl until they hold their shape. Add the remaining sweetener and beat again until you have a thick, glossy meringue.

Spread the meringue over the lemon filling and return to the oven for 5–6 minutes, until golden brown.

Per serving: 245 calories; 4g protein; 14g fat; 4.6g saturated fat; 27g carbohydrates; 5.2g sugar; 0.7g fiber; 0.11g sodium

plum muesli crumble with custard

SERVES 4

1 pound, 10 ounces red plums, quartered and pitted

½ cup Splenda granulated sweetener

2 tablespoons orange juice

1½ tablespoons butter

1⅓ cups muesli

¼ cup marzipan, coarsely grated

for the custard:

2 tablespoons custard powder

2½ cups lowfat milk

2–3 tablespoons Splenda granulated sweetener

This recipe uses a very clever crumble topping, simply made by mixing good-quality muesli with melted butter and some grated marzipan. For the topping, custard powder may be replaced with ready-made custard.

Preheat the oven to 375°F.

Put the plums into a baking dish and sprinkle with three quarters of the sweetener and with the orange juice. Toss to coat, then bake in the oven for 15 minutes while you prepare the topping.

Melt the butter and mix in the muesli, the remaining sweetener, and the grated marzipan. Remove the baking dish from the oven and sprinkle the muesli topping over the plums in an even layer.

Place back in the oven and bake for 10–15 minutes, until the plums are tender and the topping is crunchy and golden brown.

To make the custard, put the custard powder into a saucepan with ¼ cup of the milk and stir until blended. Add the remaining milk over a low heat, stirring constantly until smooth and thickened. Stir in sweetener to taste, and serve with the crumble.

Per serving: 489 calories; 11g protein; 18g fat; 8.6g saturated fat; 76g carbohydrates; 51.9g sugar; 6.1g fiber; 0.32g sodium

orange and raisin semolina puddings

SERVES 2

¼ cup ground semolina

2 cups lowfat milk

3 tablespoons sultanas or golden raisins

2 tablespoons Splenda granulated
  sweetener

½ teaspoon vanilla extract

pinch ground nutmeg or cinnamon

2 oranges

2 eggs, beaten

I've given this classic milk dessert a new interpretation.

Preheat the oven to 375°F. Put the semolina into a saucepan and blend in the milk. Heat, stirring constantly, until thickened and smooth. Cook gently for another 2–3 minutes, then remove from the heat.

Add the raisins, sweetener, vanilla extract, and ground nutmeg or cinnamon to the semolina and grate into it the zest of 1 orange, using a fine grater. Squeeze the zested orange into the pan and stir together. Taste, adding a little extra sweetener if you like. Stir in the eggs and divide between two individual heatproof dishes. Bake in the oven—use a toaster oven if you have one—for 10 minutes, or until just set.

Meanwhile, peel the remaining orange and cut into slices with a sharp, serrated knife.

Arrange the orange slices on top of the baked puddings. Bake for another 5–6 minutes, until golden brown. Serve at once.

Per serving: 346 calories; 18g protein; 10g fat; 3.9g saturated fat; 48g carbohydrates; 32.2g sugar; 2.1g fiber; 0.18g sodium

gooseberry and elderflower compote

SERVES 6

5 elderflower heads

2 tablespoons Splenda granulated
  sweetener

1½ pounds gooseberries, topped and
  tailed (about 5½-6 cups)

You may have to hunt for fresh gooseberries—try farmers' markets for a start, in the summer when they're in season.

Tie the elderflower heads together with a piece of string.

Put 1¼ cups of water into a saucepan and stir in the sweetener. Add the gooseberries and elderflower heads. Simmer for about 15 minutes or until the gooseberries are cooked. Remove and discard the elderflowers.

Eat the gooseberry and elderflower compote hot or cold. Try serving it with cream or ice cream. To make into a "fool", fold in ⅔ cup lightly whipped cream or a mixture of cream and custard.

Per serving: 40 calories; 1g protein; 0g fat; 0g saturated fat; 8g carbohydrates; 8.2g sugar; 2.7g fiber; 0g sodium

granola and raspberry crunch

SERVES 4

for the granola:

¾ stick (1½ cups) unsalted butter, cut into cubes, plus extra for greasing

2⅓ cups rolled oats (old-fashioned oats)

¼ tablespoons slivered almonds

2 tablespoons unsalted macadamia nuts, chopped

2 tablespoons hazelnuts, skins removed and roughly chopped

2 tablespoons brazil nuts, roughly chopped

2 tablespoons Splenda granulated sweetener

2 teaspoons grated orange zest

pinch of grated nutmeg

pinch of ground cloves

pinch of ground cinnamon

3 tablespoons golden syrup (or corn syrup or honey)

2½ tablespoons dried apricots, finely chopped

2½ tablespoons dates, finely chopped

2½ tablespoons dried cherries

2½ tablespoons golden raisins

2 heaping cups Greek-style yogurt

2 cups fresh raspberries

It's lovely to make your own granola, and it can be used in so many ways—in this dessert, over your breakfast yogurt, or even as a crunchy, nutritious snack. You'll be happy to find you have some leftovers after you've made this recipe...

Preheat the oven to 325°F. Lightly grease two shallow baking trays with a little butter.

First of all, make the granola. Mix the rolled oats, nuts, sweetener, orange zest, and spices together. Melt the butter and golden syrup in a large saucepan. Add the oat mixture and combine well. Pour this into the prepared tray. Pat the mixture down and bake in the oven for 15–20 minutes.

Remove from the oven, turn the second buttered tray upside-down and place over the hot tray. Holding the trays together, turn them upside-down so the granola falls into the fresh tray. Pat the granola down firmly again and return to the oven for a further 20–25 minutes or until golden brown.

Let the granola cool completely. Once cool, the granola will have become brittle. Break into small chunks and weigh out 8 ounces for the dessert (about 1½-2 cups). (You'll have some leftovers that can be stored in an airtight container.)

Fold the granola and dried fruits into the yogurt. Scoop into a glass bowl, top with the fresh raspberries, and serve.

Per serving: 388 calories; 6g protein; 24g fat; 10.8g saturated fat; 38g carbohydrates; 23.4g sugar; 5g fiber; 0.03g sodium

yorkshire curd tart

SERVES 6

for the pie crust:

1¹/₃ cups flour

pinch of salt

3 tablespoons cold butter, cut into cubes,
   plus extra for greasing

3 tablespoons shortening (for
   dough-making), cut into cubes

2 teaspoons Splenda granulated
   sweetener

for the filling:

2 eggs

¼ cup light cream

1 cup plain cottage cheese

3 tablespoons Splenda granulated
   sweetener

½ teaspoon vanilla extract

¹/₃ cup currants

finely grated zest of 1 lemon

pinch ground nutmeg

Fresh dairy ingredients are the heroes of this fabulous Yorkshire favorite. It's wonderful to make the pie crust yourself, but if you're short of time, you can use a store-bought all-butter pie crust instead.

Sift the flour and salt into a large mixing bowl. Rub in the butter and shortening with your fingertips until the mixture resembles fine breadcrumbs. Stir in the sweetener, then add enough chilled water to make a firm dough. Knead lightly for a few moments then wrap in plastic wrap or waxed paper and refrigerate for about 10 minutes.

Preheat the oven to 400°F.

Roll out the dough on a lightly floured surface and use to line a 9-inch pie plate or quiche pan. Prick the bottom, line with tinfoil, and bake blind (without the filling) for 10 minutes. Remove the tinfoil and cool slightly. Reduce the oven temperature to 350°F.

For the filling, beat the eggs and cream together in a mixing bowl. Add the cottage cheese, sweetener, vanilla extract, currants, and lemon zest. Pour into the pie shell and sprinkle with the ground nutmeg.

Bake for 30–35 minutes, until the filling has set and turned a light golden brown. Serve warm.

Per serving: 308 calories; 10g protein; 17g fat; 8g saturated fat; 31g carbohydrates; 8.6g sugar; 1.1g fiber ; 0.29g sodium

italian fruit trifle

SERVES 8

12 ladyfingers, broken in half

8 amaretti cookies (e.g. Amaretti di Saronno) or 15 small almond macaroons, lightly crushed

1/3 cup plus 2 teaspoons marsala

9 ounces strawberries, hulled and sliced (about 1¾-2 cups)

finely grated zest and juice of 2 oranges

2 tablespoons Splenda granulated sweetener

2 cups blueberries

1 cup mascarpone cheese

2/3 cup heavy cream

This trifle is perfect for a dinner party—it's easy to whip up and your guests will love the sensational flavors.

Put the ladyfingers in the bottom of a glass bowl with most of the amaretti or almond macaroons. Sprinkle evenly with the marsala, then scatter most of the strawberries over the top.

Put the orange juice and sweetener into a saucepan and heat until simmering. Add most of the blueberries and simmer gently for 1 minute. Remove from the heat and cool, then spoon into the trifle dish.

Beat the mascarpone cheese until softened, then whisk in the cream and orange zest. Spoon into the trifle dish, spreading it out to cover the fruit.

Decorate the trifle with the reserved cookies, blueberries and strawberries. Cover and refrigerate until ready to serve.

Per serving: 353 calories; 3g protein; 28g fat; 16.6g saturated fat; 21g carbohydrates; 14.7g sugar; 1.1g fiber; 0.08g sodium

little "summer puddings"

SERVES 4

1¾ cups blueberries

3 tablespoons Splenda granulated
   sweetener

5 ounces strawberries, hulled and sliced
   (about 1 cup)

5 ounces raspberries (about 1¼ cups)

6 slices mediumsliced white bread

A British "summer pudding" is a refreshing dessert made of summer berries in a glass bowl lined with white bread, which is dyed a purply-red from the fruit juices. Out of season, just thaw some frozen summer fruits instead. This recipe makes individual mini-puddings.

Put the blueberries and sweetener into a saucepan with 1 tablespoon of cold water. Cook gently until juice just begins to run from the fruit–this will take about 2–3 minutes. Remove from the heat and add the strawberries and raspberries. Let cool.

Cut out circles from the bread, using cookie cutters, to fit into four individual ovenproof bowls. You need four circles of about 2 inches, four circles of about 2½ inches and four of about 3 inches.

Put the small bread circles into the bottom of each bowl. Spoon half the fruit mixture into the bowls. Place the medium-sized bread circles on top, then spoon in the remaining fruit. Top with the large bread circles, then spoon any remaining fruit juice over it. Cover with plastic wrap and refrigerate for several hours, or overnight.

To serve, run a knife around the inside of each bowl and turn out the puddings onto individual plates. Great served with light cream or yogurt.

Per serving: 200 calories; 6g protein; 1g fat; 0g saturated fat; 44g carbohydrates; 10.1g sugar; 3.4g fiber; 0.35g sodium

"queen of puddings"

SERVES 4

2 teaspoons butter

1½ cups fresh white breadcrumbs

2 cups milk

½ teaspoon vanilla extract

3 tablespoons Splenda granulated
  sweetener

2 large eggs, separated

2 tablespoons raspberry jam

"Queen of puddings" is another classic British dessert, this one with a custard-breadcrumb base and jam and baked meringue. Serve it straight from the oven.

Preheat the oven to 350°F. Grease a 5-cup baking dish with a little of the butter. Sprinkle the breadcrumbs into the baking dish.

Heat the milk, remaining butter, and vanilla extract until just lukewarm—take care that the mixture does not get too hot. Remove from the heat and add 2 tablespoons of the sweetener. Beat in the egg yolks. Pour into the baking dish, mix with the breadcrumbs, then let soak for 15–20 minutes.

Bake in the oven for 20–25 minutes, until set. Remove the baking dish from the oven and let cool slightly.

Beat the egg whites in a grease-free bowl until they hold their shape, then add the remaining sweetener and beat again until you have a thick, glossy meringue. Spread the jam over the baked pudding, then pile the meringue on top. Bake for another 5–8 minutes, until golden brown.

Per serving: 208 calories; 10g protein; 8g fat; 3.3g saturated fat; 26g carbohydrates; 12.4g sugar; 0.4g fiber; 0.25g sodium

hot and cold drinks

kiwi and raspberry smoothie

SERVES 2

4 kiwis

**12 ounces fresh, ripe raspberries
(about 3 cups)**

2 tablespoons yogurt

**1 tablespoon Splenda granulated
sweetener**

Peel and roughly chop the kiwis. Place the raspberries, kiwis, yogurt, and sweetener into a blender and blitz until smooth.

Taste and adjust the sweetness to your liking. Chill in the refrigerator for 30 minutes and serve decorated with some extra raspberries or kiwi slices if you like.

Per serving: 62 calories; 3g protein; 1g fat; 0.1g saturated fat; 12g carbohydrates; 11.9g sugar; 3.3g fiber; 0.02g sodium

tropical fruit smoothie

SERVES 2

1 banana

1 cup strawberries

¹/₃ mango

1 papaya, peeled and thinly sliced

²/₃ cup orange juice

1 tablespoon honey

**1 tablespoon Splenda granulated
sweetener**

1 tablespoon lemon juice

Peel the banana and slice in half lengthwise. Hull the strawberries and cut them in half from top to tip. Peel and pit the mango, and cube one third of its flesh. Peel the papaya and scoop out the seeds, then slice the flesh.

Lay all the fruits on a small baking tray and freeze for about 2 hours until solid, but not deep-frozen.

Put the fruits into a blender with the remaining ingredients and blitz to a puree. Pour into tall glasses and chill before serving.

Per serving: 186 calories; 2g protein; 1g fat; 0.1g saturated fat; 46g carbohydrates; 44.5g sugar; 5.2g fiber; 0.02g sodium

mexican hot chocolate

SERVES 4

2 cups whole milk
5 ounces Mexican chocolate, broken into
    pieces (a scant cup)
½ tablespoon Splenda granulated
    sweetener

Mexico is the home of chocolate and has many varieties available. Good, dark, unsweetened chocolate can be melted into the most delicious of drinks—warming in winter and very addictive. Use the best quality chocolate you can find.

Put the milk and chocolate pieces into a large saucepan and add 2 cups of water. Place over a low heat and stir until the chocolate is completely melted.

Continue to stir, bringing the mixture to almost simmering point. Keep it there for about 5 minutes for the flavors to develop.

Add the sweetener and stir in well, cooking the hot chocolate for a minute longer. Remove from the heat and pour into a blender. Blitz until frothy, then pour into four good-sized mugs. Now drink!

Per serving: 295 calories; 7g protein; 20g fat; 10.8g saturated fat; 23g carbohydrates; 16.5g sugar; 2.2g fiber; 0.05g sodium

sloe gin

MAKES 5 CUPS

1 pound, 12 ounces sloes or other tart
   small plums
1 cup sugar
5 cups gin
1/3 cup plus 2 teaspoons Splenda
   granulated sweetener

Sloe gin is best left for a year before drinking, if you can bear to, although it doesn't taste bad that first Christmas! You can make this with sloes, which taste very bitter, or with another tart plum. Regular sloe gin does need some sugar to develop the alcohol; however this version, with reduced sugar and added sweetener, works well, too.

Wash the fruit and dry thoroughly. Prick the sloes in several places with a needle and put them into a sterilized glass jar (see page 76).

Add the sugar and pour in the gin. Seal the jar tightly and leave for 2–3 months, shaking every couple of days at first, and when you remember later on. It will be ready to bottle then, at which time you should strain the gin, stir in the sweetener, and bottle the liquid. The more it matures, the richer the flavors that develop, so try and leave it for another year.

Per 25ml serving: 76 calories; 0g protein; 0g fat; 0g saturated fat; 6g carbohydrates; 5.6g sugar; 0g fiber; 0g sodium

mulled wine

SERVES 8

1 bottle dry red wine

$^1\!/_3$ cup plus 1 teaspoon Splenda granulated
sweetener

½ cup brandy

2 cinnamon sticks

6 whole cloves

pinch of grated nutmeg

2 oranges, thinly sliced

1 lemon, thinly sliced

Variations of this drink can be found around the world, from Sweden to Germany, from Moldova to Mexico. It's a warming drink, perfect for winter parties.

Place the ingridients in a large, heavy pan and add ½ cup of water. Place over a low heat and gently bring to a simmer, stirring occasionally to bruise the fruit. Once the sweetener is dissolved and the mixture fragrant, remove from the heat and serve.

Per serving: 111 calories; 0g protein; 0g fat; 0g saturated fat; 3g carbohydrates; 2.8g sugar; 0.3g fiber; 0.01g sodium

elderflower syrup

MAKES ABOUT 5 CUPS

$^1\!/_3$ cup plus 2 teaspoons Splenda
granulated sweetener

12 elderflower heads

4 unwaxed lemons

Into a heavy saucepan pour 5 cups of cold water, add the sweetener, and place over a medium heat and dissolve the sweetener. Gently stir in the elderflower heads with a wooden spoon. Bring the liquid to a boil and cook for about 5 minutes. Meanwhile, grate the zest from the lemons and then squeeze out the juice. Add the zest and juice to the pan and stir well. Continue to boil for a 1 minute longer, then remove the pan from the heat. Let it cool and infuse for 24 hours.

Strain the mixture through a double thickness of cheesecloth and bottle it. Store in a cool place–it should keep for 1–2 months. Dilute to the strength required.

Per 2-tablespoon serving: 11 calories; 0g protein; 0g fat; 0g saturated fat; 3g carbohydrates; 2.8g sugar; 0g fiber; 0g sodium

sweet geranium leaf lemonade

SERVES 6

2 large handfuls of young sweet
   geranium leaves
½ cup Splenda granulated sweetener
juice of 3 unwaxed lemons
about 3 cups sparkling water

Sweet geraniums (*Pelargonium graveolens*) have divinely fragrant leaves and flowers in summer. There are many different varieties, from the delicately pink-flowered *Pelargonium* "Attar of Roses" to the white-flowered *Pelargonium odoratissimum*. They make a magnificent flavored lemonade with a difference.

Hold the sweet geranium leaves over a big, stainless steel pan. Crush them in your fist to bruise them slightly—this will bring out the scent—and drop them into the pan.

Add the sweetener and 2½ cups of tap water and heat gently and slowly. Bring the water just to boiling point and simmer for 3 minutes or so. Remove from the heat, stir in the lemon juice, and let cool.

When cold, dilute with sparkling water to taste. Chill and serve with ice cubes.

Per serving: 62 calories; 0g protein; 0g fat; 0g saturated fat; 17g carbohydrates; 16.3g sugar; 0g fiber; 0g sodium

strawberry syrup

SERVES 2

2 cups ripe strawberries, hulled
2 tablespoons Splenda granulated
   sweetener
juice of ½ lemon, strained

This is a truly refreshing recipe which makes a change from lemonade on hot summer days. Pick the strawberries when they are really ripe and red all over—this syrup will taste so much better for it!

Place the strawberries and sweetener in a blender with ⅔ cup of water and blitz to a puree.

Strain the puree through a fine mesh strainer and place it in a jelly bag suspended over a bowl. Let it drip through and, when the pulp in the jelly bag is dry, add another 1¼ cups of water and let this drip through as well.

Mix in the strained lemon juice and dilute with iced water to taste.

Per serving: 36 calories; 1g protein; 0g fat; 0g saturated fat; 8g carbohydrates; 8.4g sugar; 1.2g fiber; 0.01g sodium

halloween punch

SERVES 10

6 large apples, unpeeled, cored,
  and cut up
4 cups hard cider
1 tablespoon Splenda granulated
  sweetener
3 cinnamon sticks
3 star anise
1 cup dark rum

This rum and cider punch is hugely comforting to drink on a crisp autumn evening around Halloween time. It goes well with a good slab of porter cake (see page 68) and is best made 24 hours before serving so that the flavors really do get the chance to mingle.

Put everything but the rum into a large pot. Add 4 cups of water and bring just to the boil, stirring well. Turn the heat down and simmer for 1¼ hours.

Pour in the rum and continue to simmer for 1 minute or so. Remove from the heat and set aside to cool. Serve either warm or cold—just make sure the mixture doesn't come to a boil when you reheat it.

Per serving: 134 calories; 0g protein; 0g fat; 0g saturated fat; 13g carbohydrates; 13.4g sugar; 1.6g fiber; 0.01g sodium

christmas punch

SERVES 15

3 bottles red wine
¼ cup Splenda granulated sweetener
3 cloves
pinch of nutmeg
1–1½ cinnamon sticks
1¼ cups dark rum
zest and juice of 1 lemon
zest and juice of 3 oranges

It's always fun to get all the family involved in making the Christmas punch. The spices fill the house with their delicious aromas. This recipe will serve 15 people, if you're not too greedy!

Put the red wine, sweetener, cloves, nutmeg, cinnamon sticks, rum, and add just the zest from the lemon and oranges into a large, stainless steel pot. Warm it gently until it just reaches simmering point, then add the lemon and orange juice. Continue cooking for a couple of minutes, then let cool slightly and serve in tall tumblers.

Per serving: 153 calories; 0g protein; 0g fat; 0g saturated fat; 2g carbohydrates; 1.9g sugar; 0g fiber; 0.01g sodium

conversion chart

Weight (solids)

7g	¼ oz.	370g	13 oz.
10g	⅓ oz.	400g	14 oz.
20g	¾ oz.	425g	15 oz.
30g	1 oz.	450g	1lb,16 oz.
40g	1½ oz.	500g (½kg)	18 oz.
55g	2 oz.	600g	1¼ lb.
70g	2½ oz.	700g	1½ lb.
85g	3 oz.	750g	1lb. 10 oz.
100g	3½ oz.	900g	2 lb.
115g	4 oz. (¼ lb.)	1kg	2¼ lb.
125g	4½ oz.	1.1kg	2½ lb.
155g	5½ oz.	1.2kg	2¾ lb.
170g	6 oz.	1.4kg	3 lb.
200g	7 oz.	1.5kg	3¼ lb.
225g	8 oz. (½ lb.)	1.6kg	3½ lb.
255g	9 oz.	1.8kg	4 lb.
285g	10 oz.	2kg	4½ lb.
300g	10½ oz.	2.3kg	5 lb.
310g	11 oz.	2.5kg	5½ lb.
325g	11½ oz.	3kg	6½ lb.
340g	12 oz. (¾ lb.)		

A NOTE ON SELF-RISING FLOUR:

If self-rising flour is unavailable, then use all-purpose flour and add 1 teaspoon baking powder and a pinch of salt.

Volume (liquids)

5ml	1 teaspoon
15ml	1 tablespoon or ½fl oz
30ml	1fl oz. (2 tbsp.)
45ml	1½fl oz. (3 tbsp.)
60ml	2fl oz. (¼ cup)
90ml	3fl oz.
100ml	3½fl oz.
120ml	4fl oz. (½ cup)
150ml	5fl oz.
180ml	6fl oz. (¾ cup)
240ml	8fl oz. (1 cup)
300ml	10fl oz. (1¼ cups)
360ml	12fl oz. (1½ cups)
400ml	14fl oz. (1¾ cups)
480ml	16fl oz. (1 pint/2 cups)
500ml (0.5 liter)	17fl oz.
550ml	19fl oz.
600ml	20fl oz. (2½ cups)
700ml	24fl oz. (3 cups)
820ml	28fl oz. (3½ cups)
950ml	32fl oz. (1 quart/4 cups)
1 liter	34fl oz.
1.2 liters	40fl oz. (5 cups)
1.5 liters	50fl oz.
1.8 liters	60fl oz. (7½ cups)
2 liters	68fl oz. (8½ cups)

Length

5mm	¼ inch
1cm	½ inch
2cm	¾ inch
2.5cm	1 inch
3cm	1¼ inches
4cm	1½ inches
5cm	2 inches
7.5 cm	3 inches
10cm	4 inches
15cm	6 inches
18cm	7 inches
20cm	8 inches
25cm	10 inches
28cm	11 inches
30 cm	12 inches

Oven temperatures

225°F	110°C	gas mark ¼	cool
250°F	120°C	gas mark ½	very low
275°F	140°C	gas mark 1	very low
300°F	150°C	gas mark 2	low
325°F	160°C	gas mark 3	low
350°F	180°C	gas mark 4	moderately low
375°F	190°C	gas mark 5	moderately hot
400°F	200°C	gas mark 6	hot
425°F	220°C	gas mark 7	hot
450°F	230°C	gas mark 8	very hot
475°F	250°C	gas mark 9	very hot

* For fan-assisted ovens, reduce temperatures by 20-40°F (about 10-20°C), according to your oven manual

Temperature conversion

°C=(°F-32) ÷1.8
°F=(°Cx1.8) +32

index